COOKING with CANNABIS

COOKING with
CANNABIS

MORE THAN 100 DELICIOUS EDIBLES

Pat Crocker

STERLING
New York

STERLING
New York

An Imprint of Sterling Publishing Co., Inc.
1166 Avenue of the Americas
New York, NY 10036

ISBN 978-1-4549-4075-3
978-1-4549-4076-0 (e-book)

Library of Congress Cataloging-in-Publication Data

Names: Crocker, Pat, author.
Title: Cooking with cannabis : more than 100 delicious edibles / Pat Crocker.
Description: New York : Sterling Epicure, [2020] | Includes bibliographical references and index. |
    Summary: "With more than 100 recipes, this cookbook makes it easy to master the art of cooking
    with cannabis! It includes practical information on dosing, infusing, and extracting the maximum
    benefit from cannabis, as well as tips for first-time users. Every serving delivers 5mg THC, perfect
    for experiencing the recreational and gustatory pleasures of cannabis. The delicious dishes include
    a Mini Quiche with Arugula & Smoked Salmon, Canna-Sweet Potato Hummus, a Black Bean Burger,
    Asparagus-Stuffed Mushrooms, and Chocolate Truffles"-- Provided by publisher.
Identifiers: LCCN 2019058213 (print) | LCCN 2019058214 (ebook) | ISBN
    9781454940753 (trade paperback) | ISBN 9781454940760 (ebook)
Subjects: LCSH: Cooking (Marijuana) | LCGFT: Cookbooks.
Classification: LCC TX819.M25 C76 2020 (print) | LCC TX819.M25 (ebook) |
    DDC 641.6/379--dc23
LC record available at https://lccn.loc.gov/2019058213
LC ebook record available at https://lccn.loc.gov/2019058214

Distributed in Canada by Sterling Publishing Co., Inc.
c/o Canadian Manda Group, 664 Annette Street
Toronto, Ontario M6S 2C8, Canada
Distributed in the United Kingdom by GMC Distribution Services
Castle Place, 166 High Street, Lewes, East Sussex BN7 1XU, England
Distributed in Australia by NewSouth Books
University of New South Wales, Sydney, NSW 2052, Australia

For information about custom editions, special sales, and premium and corporate purchases,
please contact Sterling Special Sales at 800-805-5489 or specialsales@sterlingpublishing.com.

Manufactured in Spain

2 4 6 8 10 9 7 5 3 1

sterlingpublishing.com

Cover design by Igor Satanovsky
Interior design by Shannon Nicole Plunkett
Photography credits page 210

CONTENTS

< INTRODUCTION >

I've been developing Cannabis-specific recipes, testing them, and cooking with Cannabis for four years, and every time I work with a new strain of Cannabis or a new ratio of CBD to THC, a new experience presents itself. This book is a culmination of my adventures with Cannabis in the kitchen. It's an invitation to start experimenting and developing your own relationship with Cannabis. It is my hope that you fall in love, as I have, with the concept of cooking with and honoring this healing mother herb. As you will learn, if you read about the human endocannabinoid system in Appendix A (page 182), no other plant has the same affinity to human health through actual physical connections in our brain and body.

Because I'm a culinary herbalist, I approach Cannabis with respect and wonder at the plant's ability to improve human lives. I've capitalized the species name because this is how botanists treat the Latin names of all living organisms, so *Cannabis* is the only designation I use for this herb. You won't see words such as *marijuana*, *dope*, *mary jane*, *grass*, *bhang*, *weed*, *reefer*, *pot*, *ganja*, *joints*, *devil's lettuce*, *hash*, *blunts*, *dabs*, *wax*, *shatter*, *kine bud*, *dime*, *Maui wowie*, or *mafafa* in this book. It was the vilification and banning of this plant that earned it a thousand code names in almost as many languages, and now, after 80 years of worldwide war on the plant, we in Canada and other jurisdictions where it is legal, can use its Latin name openly and with reverence.

My background in cooking with healing herbs has also taught me to use whole herbs, not only in medicine, but also in food. When we isolate one component from a plant, we produce a drug that's not food, and herbalists agree that using the whole plant makes for more powerful herbal medicine. And medicine, albeit *delicious* medicine, is what you will be making, whether intentionally or not, when you begin to cook with Cannabis.

What you will see in the recipes is the addition of other healing herbs—herbs like cinnamon, turmeric, ginger, and garlic. As long as the taste is awesome, why wouldn't we add other calming, anti-inflammatory, or pain-fighting herbs to everyday recipes? Why wouldn't we want our food to be our medicine as the Greek physician Hippocrates (c. 460–c. 370 BCE) so wisely advised over 2,000 years ago?

< vi >

If you're new to Cannabis or Cannabis edibles, you might want to start by reading Appendix A "Cannabis Basics: Understanding the Human Endocannabinoid System" because this will give you an understanding of how Cannabis affects humans. If you just want to get into the kitchen and cook, take a look at chapter 1, "Cooking with Cannabis: Kitchen Basics" because there are some key techniques that you need to master in order to have the best experience with Cannabis edibles.

However your Cannabis-in-the-kitchen adventure unfolds, I hope you learn and develop your own responsible, fun, and tasty food experimentation with Cannabis.

Be well and eat Cannabis.

Pat Crocker

RISKS OF EARLY CANNABIS USE

It can't be emphasized enough: THC in Cannabis is strictly out of bounds for children, adolescents, and young adults (anyone under age 25). For this group, it has been shown to increase the risk of schizophrenia-like psychoses and may trigger acute schizophrenic psychosis; it may increase deficits in attention and motivation; and it may cause apathy and changes in personality, emotions, and cognitive functions. Taking THC in Cannabis when young can also negatively affect memory. All this to say, label and keep your Cannabis flower, infusions, tinctures, and edibles stored safely away from anyone under the age of 25.

CHAPTER 1

COOKING WITH CANNABIS:
< Kitchen Basics >

We live in interesting times. Those of us who happen to reside in countries or jurisdictions that have made Cannabis legal can't forget the 80-year worldwide ban, just as we can easily remember stolen moments, when a puff or a bite of a wacky brownie brought, if not a dangerous one, then certainly a forbidden thrill. Did we understand the difference between smoking and ingesting Cannabis? Did we know or care about how the plant has co-evolved with humans over centuries? Likely not.

Now that many people are transitioning—or hoping to transition—to a normal relationship with a truly helpful plant and learning how to summon the herb to do its magic, I invite you to connect with Cannabis in the kitchen. There are some easy but new techniques you'll need to master so that you can make your own Cannabis edibles, namely decarboxylating (page 6), infusing (page 9), and dosing (page 9).

Once you understand the why and how of Cannabis cooking, you can be creative and, most of all, playful with Cannabis in recipes; you can learn and experiment with different strains and ratios of CBD to THC and begin to observe how the herb can be of benefit to your health.

This, then, is the first stop on your cooking with Cannabis odyssey. Bon voyage.

< 1 >

CANNABIS-INFUSED FATS

Canna Coco Oil > 13

Canna Oil > 15

Canna Ghee > 16

Ghee > 17

YOUR FIRST CANNABIS EDIBLES TEST

Pat's Majoun Morsels > 19

CANNABIS-INFUSED
FULL-FAT DAIRY PRODUCTS

Canna Cream > 21

Canna Whipped Cream > 22

CANNABIS-INFUSED HONEY

Canna Honey > 24

Canna Healing Honey > 25

CANNABIS-INFUSED COMPOUND BUTTERS

Canna Herb Butter > 26

Ayurvedic Canna Butter > 27

Canna Miso Butter > 28

CANNABIS-INFUSED NUT BUTTERS

Canna Nut Butter > 29

Homemade Canna Nut Butter > 30

Spiced Canna Nut Butter > 31

CANNABIS-INFUSED TINCTURES

Canna Tincture (alcohol) > 33

Canna Tincture (glycerine) > 34

CANNABIS-INFUSED SIMPLE SYRUP

Lemon-Ginger Simple Syrup > 37

Raspberry-Thyme Simple Syrup > 38

Matcha-Rosemary Simple Syrup > 39

CANNABIS-INFUSED CONDIMENTS

CANNABIS-INFUSED SPICE PASTES

Canna Curry Spice Paste > 41

Canna Mediterranean Herb Paste > 42

Sweet Canna Thai Spice Paste > 43

Red-Hot Canna Curry Paste > 44

CANNABIS-INFUSED SPREADS

Canna Churri > 45

Easy Canna Mayo > 46

Canna Mayo > 47

Cannabis Leaf Pesto > 49

WHY MAKE CANNABIS EDIBLES?

Ingesting Cannabis is a different experience than smoking it, but it's certainly not a new one. Legend has it that as far back as 2000 BCE, the Indian god Shiva introduced *bhang*, an edible Cannabis drink, for the pleasure of humankind.

First up, edibles are ideal for people who don't want to damage their lungs by vaping or inhaling smoke. As with all food we make from scratch, we can control the quality of the ingredients (organic, GMO- or gluten-free) in edibles, as well as the amount of THC. Commercial edible products are designed to get you high, but be aware of the total amount of THC in edibles you purchase. Some contain a range of 10 mg to 40 mg or even higher amounts of THC, so be sure to check the label. Start low and go slow–that is, you might want to start with 1 mg and add 1 mg each time to work up to a level that feels right for you.

You can also make informed choices about the licensed producer from whom you source Cannabis for your edibles. And, most importantly, you have control over the dosage when you make your own.

RAW VERSUS DECARBOXYLATED CANNABIS

Raw Cannabis (fresh and dried) contains many cannabinoids, including THCA (tetrahydrocannabinolic acid) and CBDA (Cannabidiol). Both are the biosynthetic precursors to THC and CBD, respectively, and have vastly different properties than their heated or decarboxylated end compounds, namely, THC and CBD. For one, eating raw Cannabis, with its THCA, won't get you high.

We use heat during smoking or decarboxylating Cannabis flowers in order to burn off the acid component in THCA and CBDA, and convert them to THC and CBD. But while there needs to be much more research into the benefits of eating raw Cannabis, we do know that terpenes and flavonoids in Cannabis are diminished with heating. Flavonoids and terpenes are found in all herbs, and they're significant because they provide medicinal properties for human healing. My advice is to treat the raw Cannabis plant as you would any other edible plant: Use it often and use all parts.

Dr. William Courtney, physician and Cannabis researcher, claims that raw Cannabis is a superfood and that eating THCA and the other cannabinoids, terpenes, and flavonoids in raw Cannabis is more effective as an antioxidant, anti-inflammatory, anti-diabetic, heart muscle strengthener, and neuroprotector than consuming heated or decarboxylated Cannabis. Raw Cannabis also provides the ideal ratio of one omega-6 fatty acid to almost two omega-3 fatty acids.

TIPS FOR SAFELY ENJOYING CANNABIS EDIBLES

- Always be mindful of dose (the amount of THC in the food you are eating).

- If you are new to Cannabis, start with a very low amount of THC—1 mg—and gradually increase the dose as you begin to recognize what feels right for you. Keep in mind that the lowest effective dose is always the goal.

- The recipes in this book are designed to deliver 5 mg THC, so you can easily start with half or even a quarter of a serving. Even if you know your tolerance for Cannabis, take a 5 mg serving to begin and the next time you can decide if you want one, one and a half, or even two servings once you know how your body metabolizes edibles. I recommend that you never exceed 10 mg THC.

- Be aware that, when it is eaten, THC is absorbed through the gut and metabolized through the liver (as opposed to going directly into the bloodstream when smoked), so it will take anywhere from one to four hours for the effect to be felt.

- When THC is ingested (as opposed to being smoked or vaped), the effects may be stronger, and they may last longer.

- Everybody is different, and so is your state of mind every time you ingest an edible.

- All these factors will have an effect on how you react to THC in an edible:

  - Stress
  - Fatigue
  - Your weight
  - Your previous experiences with ingesting THC
  - The actual contents of your stomach

- **With Cannabis edibles, second helpings are not to be had, especially if you haven't given the first serving at least four hours!** So I recommend that you make two batches of a recipe for which you know you won't be able to curb your enthusiasm. If you make the second batch Cannabis-free, you can safely eat as much of it as your appetite and waistline dictate.

- Clearly label and keep edibles out of the reach of children and young adults.

The following lists compare what we now know about the benefits of THCA, CBDA, THC, and CBD.

THCA from Raw Cannabis	THC from Heated or Decarboxylated Cannabis
No psychedelic effect in humans	Produces psychedelic effects in humans
Reduces appetite	Stimulates appetite
Treats pain, inflammation, menstrual cramps, immune system disorders, and muscle spasms	Relieves pain and inflammation
Antinausea properties	Reduces nausea
Inhibits cancer growth, including prostate cancer growth	Creates a sense of relaxation and well-being
Antioxidant	Can cause anxiety in new users
Aids in treatment of neurodegenerative diseases	Induces sleep

CBDA from Raw Cannabis	CBD from Heated or Decarboxylated Cannabis
Helps prevent inflammation	Combats inflammation and pain
Helps some people with epilepsy	Suppresses seizure activity
Assists the immune system	Eases anxiety and depression
	Suppresses appetite
	Combats neurodegenerative diseases
	Combats tumors and cancer cells

USING RAW CANNABIS IN RECIPES

You can experiment with all parts of the Cannabis plant: leaves, stalk, roots, flower, and seeds. Although I don't juice or eat the roots or fibrous stalk, I chop and add them to other healing herbs, such as turmeric roots, ginger, or cinnamon, and infuse them in a medicinal oil to use topically for inflammation. You can also try my Root Beverage Blend (page 173), which uses chopped, roasted Cannabis, burdock, and dandelion roots.

Fresh leaves may be chopped and added to salads, juiced along with fruits and vegetables, or added to smoothies and teas. I've also used fresh leaves in several recipes, including Cannabis Leaf Pesto (page 49), Raw Cannabis Morning Juice (page 56), Poultice Pack for Aches (page 103), Cannabis Fruit and Vegetable Juices (pages 168–169); and Pat's Root Beverage Blend (page 173). You can also dry raw leaves and crush and fill gel caps to take THCA daily.

All seeds are nutritional powerhouses because they store nutrients for the emerging plant to sprout, and Cannabis seeds are no exception. You can add raw Cannabis seeds to any of the no-bake recipes in this book, such as No-Bake Energy Bars (page 66) and Fruit, Nut, and Seed Gems (page 91), or sprinkle them over No-Cook Morning Oatmeal (page 67).

There are no restrictions on using raw Cannabis in recipes, and I encourage you to grow your own plants and experiment with fresh leaves, stems, seeds, and roots, as well as the flowers.

I use dried female flowers for decarboxylating and infusing the recipes in this book because female flowers, besides being larger and covered in a sticky resin, are higher in cannabinoids, flavonoids, and terpenes than the smaller male flowers. Licensed producers sell only female flowers, so for best results, decarboxylate and use only female flowers in the recipes that call for activated or decarboxylated Cannabis.

HEATING AND INFUSING CANNABIS FOR USE IN RECIPES

Step 1
Decarboxylating Cannabis

As I mentioned previously, in its raw form, THCA (the precursor to THC) does not bind to the receptors in our brain, which is why a psychoactive experience cannot happen simply by eating raw fresh or raw dried Cannabis. Heating at a precise temperature for a specific time converts the THCA into psychoactive THC. This process is often referred to as *decarboxylation* because it removes the carboxyl group of compounds (the acid) from the raw plant material. I call the process of converting THCA into THC and CBDA to CBD, *activating* those cannabinoids.

Activation of THC and CBD only occurs when heat is applied either during smoking, vaping, or heating in an oven or a dedicated decarboxylation device (see Resources, page 210). My directions for activating whole or chopped dried flowers follow.

Decarboxylation reaction of Δ⁹-tetrahydrocannabinol

THCA ($C_{22}H_{30}O_4$) — decarboxylation, heat > 105°C → THC ($C_{21}H_{30}O_2$) + CO_2

The most widely used home method of activating (decarboxylating) raw Cannabis is to heat it in the oven. While there are several other legitimate but also some wild and crazy techniques that people employ—from using a toaster oven or a coffee press to boiling with water and then freezing, and using a sous vide process (immersing Cannabis in a plastic bag in boiling water)—I prefer to activate Cannabis in the oven (see my instructions below).

For people who want convenience and precision, there is an efficient and simple appliance made by Ardent, called the Nova Decarboxylator, which makes this step very easy (for more information about this appliance, see page 210).

Important: **Be sure to keep the original Cannabis container or write down the percentage of THC and CBD in the Cannabis you are activating because you will need this information to calculate the amount of carrier (fat, honey, or alcohol for tinctures) to use in step 2 (page 9).**

NOTE: Some Cannabis suppliers are now decarboxylating their products. If your cannabis has already been decarboxylated, go directly to step 2 on page 9.

Using the Oven to Activate (Decarboxylate) THC and CBD

¼ ounce (7 grams) coarsely chopped dried Cannabis flowers

1. Preheat the oven to 230°F (110°C). Position an oven rack in the center of the oven.

2. Spread the Cannabis evenly over a heatproof glass or ceramic pie plate. Loosely cover with foil and bake in the preheated oven for 40 minutes for high-THC strains or 1 hour and 10 minutes for high-CBD strains. Remove the pie plate from the oven and set it aside to cool.

Recipe Notes

- When decarboxylating, the intention is to convert THCA to THC and to maximize the THC in the Cannabis. I recommend decarboxylating using a glass or ceramic pie plate instead of a metal baking sheet because I found that glass prevents Cannabis from burning (the metal heats up more than the temperature of the oven).

- If your Cannabis is higher in CBD than THC, use the longer cooking time as indicated in the instructions above.

- Oven temperatures are widely variable—they can fluctuate 10 degrees up or down. An oven thermometer is handy for making sure that your oven temperature is 230°F (110°C).

- If using the oven, be prepared to enjoy (or not!) the enveloping odor of Cannabis as it bakes and the carboxyl group of constituents evaporates into your kitchen.

Step 2
Infusing Cooking Ingredients (Carriers) with Cannabis

Okay, you've activated ¼ ounce (7 grams) of precious Cannabis, and now you want to cook with it. Of course, you can grind decarboxylated Cannabis and sprinkle some of the powder into a brownie mix or toss it with a bag of nuts . . . but that isn't the best way to safely enjoy it.

In order to make incredible edibles with a specific dose of THC in every serving, the next step is to infuse decarboxylated Cannabis into a carrier, such as coconut oil, olive oil, avocado oil, ghee made from butter, cream, honey, nut butter, or alcohol by using the table below to measure the amount of carrier you need to use, based on the level of THC in your strain of Cannabis.

As you can see from the table, to calculate the amount of carrier ingredient to use, you need to know the percentage of THC that is in the strain of Cannabis you have decarboxylated. As the percentage of THC increases, the amount of carrier used to infuse it also increases. I recommend that you always use ¼ ounce (7 grams) of decarboxylated Cannabis, but you can double the amount of Cannabis as long as you double the amount of carrier in order to keep the dose at 5 mg of THC. If you double the amount of Cannabis (that is, use ½ ounce [14 grams]) and keep the amount of carrier the same as in the table, one teaspoon will deliver 10 mg of THC.

If you grow your own Cannabis and therefore may not know the percentage of THC in it, start by assuming that the percentage is at least 15 percent. After gauging the effect of your first edible, you will know if your strain is higher or lower in THC, and you can adjust the amount of carrier to use in order to get more or less THC in each serving.

Recommended Carrier Amounts by Percent (%) THC

Amount of THC	Amount of Cannabis	Amount of Carrier to Use
0% to 6% THC	¼ ounce (7 grams)	1½ to 2 cups
7% to 13% THC	¼ ounce (7 grams)	2½ to 3 cups
14% to 15% THC	¼ ounce (7 grams)	3½ to 4 cups
16% to 20% THC	¼ ounce (7 grams)	4½ cups to 5 cups

DOSE: Using the above amounts to infuse a carrier yields 5 mg THC per teaspoon.

TRACKING YOUR CANNABIS EXPERIENCE

I find it helpful to keep a log of every strain and infusion I make. It's a simple list of basic information, but it is helpful if you want to experiment with different strains and ratios of CBD to THC to track how they affect you.

Date: _____

Name of Strain and Producer: _____

Percentage THC: _____

Percentage CBD: _____

Recipe, page #: _____

Time of Day: _____

Full or Empty Stomach: _____

Mood: _____

Effect of one 5 mg THC serving: _____

IS THC LOST IN SMOKING OR BAKING?

Aside from the fact that it's difficult to control the dose when you smoke—and, more importantly, smoking isn't kind to your lungs—it's also the least efficient method of consuming THC. This is because, when you smoke, 60–80 percent of THC is lost due to burning and side-stream smoke.

You also lose THC in baking or cooking with Cannabis-infused carriers, but at a lower rate—about 50 percent. And if you make my smoothies and other recipes that don't require cooking, there is no loss of THC. So recipes using activated Cannabis are most efficient and effective if the ingredients aren't cooked.

This efficiency in maintaining THC may partially explain why edibles produce a stronger effect than smoking and why the effect lasts longer.

ADDING OTHER HEALING HERBS TO RECIPES

Medical herbalists use power herbs alone and in tandem to help alleviate symptoms such as inflammation, pain, and insomnia. So, in addition to Cannabis, I've included power herbs in some of the recipes in this book.

See Resources (page 210) for a list of online and brick-and-mortar sources for purchasing power herbs.

FOUR ESSENTIAL THINGS TO CONSIDER BEFORE YOU BEGIN WITH EDIBLES

1. Follow serving sizes and guidelines.

When making the infused oils and other carriers in this chapter, follow the Recommended Carrier Amounts table (page 9) so that every batch of Cannabis-infused carrier delivers roughly 5 mg in one teaspoon. Using this as the constant, I've worked out how much infused carrier to use in the recipes so that each serving delivers roughly 5 mg of THC.

Follow the recipe ingredient amounts and serving instructions so that you get the correct dose in every serving. Only consume one serving and always wait for a minimum of three hours before having another serving.

2. Give the edible time to work its magic.

Depending on your age, weight, metabolism, and what you had to eat prior to consuming a Cannabis edible, it could take 30 minutes to 4 hours for the THC to take effect. Eating Cannabis on an empty stomach will hasten your body's response time.

3. Be aware of the time of day when you consume the Cannabis-infused edible.

An indica-dominant strain with a higher ratio of CBD to THC works best when consumed one to two hours before bedtime, when the mind and body are ready for sleep, although it could also be eaten during the day without drastic mind-altering effects.

On the other hand, if consumed during the daytime or in a social setting when your energy level is high, the effects of a sativa-dominant strain with a higher ratio of THC to CBD could be heightened.

4. Try microdosing.

The maximum recommended dose of THC is 10 mg (less if you are just starting to experiment with THC), but it's becoming clear through patient feedback that smaller doses—so-called microdoses—may be more effective in managing the symptoms of certain conditions. When you take small amounts, between 1 and 5 mg THC, you not only lessen the psychoactive effects and still enjoy the medicinal benefits, but you may find that pain and insomnia are reduced the same amount or even more than when you take 10 mg or larger doses. Again, it's up to you to enjoy and keep track of your Cannabis adventure and determine what works for you.

A very good recipe to test the technique of microdosing is No-Bake Energy Bars (page 66) because one bar provides 2.5 mg THC. Most of the recipes in this book deliver roughly 5 mg THC. If you wish to experiment with microdosing, start with one-quarter to one-half serving and note your reactions in your log (see page 10).

ABOUT THE RECIPES

Trust me: Cooking with Cannabis is not the same as cooking with alcohol. For one thing, when heated, alcohol burns away, leaving the flavor with none of the side effects. Very early in my experimentation with Cannabis in recipes, I learned to be mindful of dose and I realized that "single-serve," stand-alone recipes are the very best types of recipes for cooking with Cannabis. That's why the recipes in this book make servings that can be measured using a standard measuring cup, tablespoon, teaspoon, or ruler to ensure that they provide roughly 5 mg THC. You won't find soups or roasted meats, stews, or desserts that are spooned out because these kinds of recipes allow for too much error in measuring the amount (dose) of THC.

The easiest way to ensure a consistent dose of THC is as follows:

1. Use the Recommended Carrier Amounts table (page 9), so that you start with a specific, known amount in the Cannabis-infused ingredients every time you infuse a carrier.

2. Make sure the Cannabis-infused carrier is blended or uniformly mixed into the dish.

3. Carefully follow the measurement of every serving so that you can be safe in assuming that one serving yields about 5 mg THC.

Canna Coco Oil

Canna Coco Oil

Cannabis-Infused Coconut Oil

Melted extra-virgin coconut oil (see Recommended Carrier Amounts table, page 9, to determine how much oil to use)

¼ ounce (7 grams) roughly chopped activated Cannabis flower (page 8)

1 serving = 1 teaspoon

DOSE: 1 teaspoon Canna Coco Oil provides about 5 mg THC if you have used the Recommended Carrier Amounts table (page 9).

STORAGE: Canna Coco Oil will keep at room temperature for 1 year or longer. Note that at temperatures above 76°F (24°C) coconut oil will be a liquid.

1. Pour coconut oil into a small (4- to 8-cup) slow cooker. Stir in Cannabis, cover, and heat on low for 4 hours, stirring once or twice. Unplug the slow cooker and set aside, covered with a lid, for 1 hour or until the crock insert is cool enough to handle. Check the temperature of the oil every 15 to 20 minutes to be sure that it does not exceed 245°F (118°C), and if it does, unplug the slow cooker to bring the temperature down.

2. Line a fine-mesh strainer with 2 or 3 layers of cheesecloth or a basket-style paper coffee filter. Set the strainer over a 2-cup measuring cup and pour the infused oil from the crock through the strainer. Be patient and let the oil drip through without squeezing or pressing on the filter (see Recipe Note below). Reserve the solids for another use (see the sidebar, "Waste Not," on page 14) or discard, being careful that children or pets cannot access it.

3. Transfer the Canna Coco Oil to a 2-cup jar with a lid. Seal, label, and store at room temperature, out of the reach of children.

Recipe Note

- Squeezing or pressing on the plant material in the strainer results in cloudy oil, and the presence of plant material may cause the oil to spoil over time.

WHY USE COCONUT OIL TO INFUSE CANNABIS?

Cold-pressed, extra-virgin coconut oil is my preference for cooking and infusing with Cannabis for this reason: Cannabinoids are fat-soluble. The fatty acids in coconut oil are saturated, which makes it the best plant-based fat for infusing cannabinoids because there are more fatty acids in coconut oil, making coconut oil extractions more potent in cannabinoids than when olive oil or avocado oil is used.

Although the American Heart Association has warned against coconut oil as a saturated fat, almost half (49 percent) of the fatty acids in coconut oil are, in fact, lauric acid, which helps lower LDL (bad) cholesterol and increase HDL (good) cholesterol.

Coconut oil is easy to use when making personal care salves and creams because it remains solid below 76°F (24°C) without the addition of beeswax.

WASTE NOT:
Save and Use Strained Cannabis

There's a lot of active THC and CBD in the leftover plant material after you've strained it from basic oils and tinctures. You can reserve and use these solids in other recipes, such as Calming Latte (page 167) or Canna-Cocoa (page 174).

To save this valuable Cannabis, set the strainer and cheesecloth with the solids in a bowl in the refrigerator for 30 minutes. Scrape the Cannabis and any solidified oil from the bowl, cheesecloth, and strainer into a jar. Seal, label, and store the jar in the refrigerator, out of the reach of children, and use within 2 weeks.

Add 1 teaspoon strained Cannabis solids to smoothies or other recipes, or heat 1 to 2 tablespoons with 6 cups or more of water or milk in tea or latte drinks and strain before serving.

Note: You can substitute strained Cannabis solids for Cannabis-infused fats, tinctures, or cream, but do not add Cannabis plant solids to dishes that already contain Cannabis.

Canna Oil

Cannabis-Infused Olive Oil or Avocado Oil

Extra-virgin olive or avocado oil (see Recommended Carrier Amounts table, page 9, to determine quantity; also see Recipe Notes, below)

¼ ounce (7 grams) roughly chopped activated Cannabis flower (page 8)

---

1 serving = 1 teaspoon

DOSE: 1 teaspoon Canna Oil provides about 5 mg THC, if you have used the Recommended Carrier Amounts table (page 9).

STORAGE: Infused olive oil will keep for up to 2 months in the refrigerator. Infused avocado oil will keep for 6 months in a cool, dark place or in the refrigerator for up to 9 months. Bring infused oil to room temperature before using it.

---

1. Pour the oil into a small (4- to 8-cup) slow cooker. Stir in the Cannabis, cover the pot, and heat on low for 1 to 2 hours, stirring once or twice. Check the temperature of the oil every half hour to be sure that it does not exceed 245°F (118°C); if it does, unplug the slow cooker to bring the temperature down.

2. Unplug the slow cooker and set it aside, covered with the lid, for 1 hour or until the crock insert is cool enough to handle.

3. Line a fine-mesh strainer with 2 or 3 layers of cheesecloth or a basket-style paper coffee filter. Set the strainer over a 2-cup measuring cup and pour the infused oil from the crock through the strainer into the measuring cup. Be patient and let the oil drip through without squeezing or pressing on the filter (see Recipe Note, page 13). Reserve solids for another use (see "Waste Not," page 14) or discard them, being careful that children or pets cannot access them.

4. Transfer the Canna Oil to a 2-cup (or larger) jar with a lid. Seal, label, and store the Canna Oil in the refrigerator, out of the reach of children.

Recipe Notes

- Always use extra-virgin coconut oil, olive oil, or avocado oil—all are high in antioxidants and vitamin E, which lower oxidation and thus deter the breakdown of nutrients during cooking.

- Olive oil is a mix of fatty acids: 73% monounsaturated, 11% polyunsaturated, and 14% saturated. Its smoke point (468°F to 485°F [242°C to 252°C]) is similar to that of ghee, which means it won't break down if it is heated to a moderately high temperature. Always store olive oil in the refrigerator.

- If you plan to use Canna Oil for high-temperature cooking, extra-virgin avocado oil is the better choice because its smoke point, 520°F (271°C), is higher than that of olive oil. The fats in avocado oil are 67% monounsaturated, 12% polyunsaturated, and 7% saturated.

Canna Ghee

Cannabis-Infused Clarified Butter

NOTE: Before you can infuse butter, you first need to make Ghee by heating it until the solids separate from the fats. Once strained, the result is clarified butter or ghee, a stable fat that can be safely stored without refrigeration. Commercially prepared ghee is available at some supermarkets and stores that sell health products (or see my recipe for ghee below). If you use store-bought ghee, be sure to use the suggested amount in the Recommended Carrier Amounts table.

Ghee (see Recommended Carrier Amounts table, page 9, to determine quantity and follow the recipe for making Ghee, opposite, or use store-bought)

¼ ounce (7 grams) roughly chopped activated Cannabis flower (page 8)

1 serving = 1 teaspoon

DOSE: 1 teaspoon Canna Ghee provides about 5 mg THC if you have used the Recommended Carrier Amounts table (page 9).

STORAGE: Canna Ghee will keep for up to 2 months at a cool room temperature or up to 4 months in the refrigerator.

1. Pour ghee into a small (4- to 8-cup) slow cooker. Stir in Cannabis, cover with the lid, and heat on low for 4 hours, stirring once or twice. Unplug the slow cooker and set it aside, covered, for 1 hour or until the crock insert is cool enough to handle.

2. Line a fine-mesh strainer with 2 or 3 layers of cheesecloth or a paper coffee filter. Set the strainer over a 2-cup measuring cup and pour the infused oil from the slow cooker through the strainer into the measuring cup. Be patient and let the ghee drip through without squeezing or pressing on the filter (see Recipe Note, page 13). Reserve the solids for another use (see "Waste Not," page 14) or discard them, being careful that children or pets cannot access them.

3. Transfer the Canna Ghee to a 2-cup jar with a lid. Seal, label, and store it at room temperature, out of the reach of children.

Recipe Note

- If your Cannabis is high in THC, you may need to double the ghee recipe (follow the Recommended Carrier Amounts table, page 9, to determine the amount of ghee you need).

GHEE

Clarified Butter

1 pound unsalted butter, cut into cubes

Recipe Notes

- Since it's made from butter, ghee is an animal product. It contains more than 400 different fatty acids, with roughly 70% being saturated, 25% monounsaturated, and about 5% polyunsaturated.

- Ghee retains fat-soluble vitamins, such as vitamins A and K. The nutty butter flavor makes it an excellent culinary fat for baking. One advantage of using butter in the form of ghee is that it remains soft at room temperature, whereas coconut oil solidifies below 76°F (24°C).

1. Place the butter in a saucepan and heat over medium-high until it has completely melted. Reduce the heat to medium and simmer the butter for about 4 minutes or until it foams. Skim off and discard the foam, using a slotted spoon.

2. Reduce the heat to low and let the butter simmer for 6 minutes. Increase the heat to medium and boil for 3 minutes or until the butter foams again. Remove the pan from the heat. Skim off and discard any remaining foam and set the pan aside for 5 minutes to cool slightly.

3. Line a fine-mesh strainer with 2 or 3 layers of cheesecloth or a basket-style paper coffee filter. Set the strainer over a 2-cup measuring cup and pour the ghee through the strainer (it will be clear and bright gold in color). Set the cup aside to cool completely and discard the whey solids.

YOUR FIRST CANNABIS EDIBLES TEST

Cooking with Cannabis begins as a kind of science experiment. However, once you understand the key issues of decarboxylating, infusing, and dosing, it quickly morphs into a creative adventure. So if you want to learn firsthand about how your body responds to homemade Cannabis edibles, I've developed an easy and delicious first test for your own infused Cannabis oil. You can use Canna Ghee or Canna Oil in this recipe, but for reasons mentioned earlier, I prefer Canna Coco Oil.

This is my favorite recipe to demonstrate how to use a Cannabis-infused fat. It's easy and quick, and, as long as you infuse your Cannabis following my Recommended Carrier Amounts table (page 9), and measure the serving size accurately, you can easily gauge how much THC is too much or not enough for you. Here is where my suggested log (page 10) can be invaluable.

To approach this first Cannabis edibles test, I recommend that you consider where, when, and with whom you will eat your first homemade edible. We know that being in a safe and comfortable setting, alone or with someone you love and trust, is the best environment, so choose a time when you are happy (not stressed) and a place that offers a calm and affable atmosphere, where you know you won't be disturbed for several hours.

Here's how: Eat only one Majoun Morsel (see recipe opposite), knowing that it will deliver about 2.5 mg THC. Wait two to four hours and actually write down any effects you feel. If you are satisfied with the results, you know that you likely will be happy consuming half of every recipe serving in this book. If you felt nothing, next time, eat two Majoun Morsels (delivering 5 mg THC in total) and record your experience. By observing and recording your experiences and only adding one Majoun Morsel or 2.5 mg THC to the dose each time, like Goldilocks, you will get very good at knowing what the perfect amount of THC is for you. This is what we mean by the caution: *Start low ... go slow.*

>>>> Pat's Majoun Morsels

1 cup whole raw almonds

½ cup pistachios or pumpkin seeds

½ cup walnut pieces

12 whole dates, pitted, or 1 cup chopped pitted

8 dried apricots

1 tablespoon chopped candied ginger

1 teaspoon ground cinnamon

1 teaspoon ground turmeric

1 teaspoon sea salt

¼ cup Canna Coco Oil (page 13)

¼ cup liquid honey

1. Combine the almonds, pistachios, walnuts, dates, apricots, and ginger in the bowl of a heavy-duty blender or food processor (see Recipe Note below) and process on high for 3 minutes or until the mixture is finely chopped.

2. Add the cinnamon, turmeric, salt, and Canna Coco Oil to the bowl. Drizzle the honey on top and process, stopping to scrape the sides of the bowl once or twice, until the mixture is thoroughly combined.

3. Using a 1-tablespoon measuring spoon, scoop the mixture, pressing against the side of the bowl to pack and level the mixture into the measuring spoon. Roll the mixture into a ball and transfer it to a parchment paper–lined baking sheet. Repeat until the whole mixture has been formed into 1-tablespoon-sized bites.

---

1 serving = 2 morsels

DOSE: 2 Majoun Morsels provide about 5 mg THC, if you have used the Recommended Carrier Amounts table (page 9) to make the Canna Coco Oil.

STORAGE: Transfer the cooled morsels to an airtight container. Label the container and keep it refrigerated for up to 1 week, out of the reach of children.

TO FREEZE: Arrange the morsels in a single layer on a baking sheet and freeze them for 30 minutes. Transfer the morsels to a resealable bag. Label the bag and keep it in the freezer for up to 4 months.

Recipe Note
- I use a powerful Ninja™ blender, which enables me to add all the ingredients to the container at once, press the ON bar, and the ingredients are quickly chopped, then coarsely ground into a homogeneous paste. If you are using a food processor or a regular blender, you may have to coarsely chop the ingredients before adding them to the container.

CANNABIS-INFUSED FULL-FAT DAIRY PRODUCTS

Because Cannabis is fat-soluble, it readily releases its cannabinoids into full-fat dairy products, such as whipping cream, full-fat ice cream, and even homogenized, full-fat milk. Canna Cream can be substituted for milk in the ice cream (page 158), and in any of the recipes for baked products in this book. You can also add a tablespoon of Canna Cream to smoothies or any hot drink. Note that this recipe provides about 10 mg THC for every tablespoon of cream.

Keep in mind that whipped cream only keeps for a very short time, so some planning must be done to ensure that the precious Cannabis is not wasted, as the cream sours (although, presumably, you could use soured Canna Cream with beet soup and in scones, or other baked products). Note also that because cream sours within days, I don't recommend that you reserve and keep any spent Cannabis.

FOR ACCURATE DOSING

It's essential that you use the Recommended Carrier Amounts table (page 9) if your Cannabis contains THC. If you are using a strain that is high in CBD with negligible THC (under 1 percent THC), you can use any amount of fat or food carrier to make it higher in CBD than 5 mg per teaspoon—the less carrier you use, the more concentrated the CBD.

>>>> Canna Cream

Heavy cream (36% butterfat; see the Recommended Carrier Amounts table page 9, to determine quantity)

¼ ounce (7 grams) roughly chopped activated Cannabis flower (page 8)

1 serving = 1 tablespoon

DOSE: 1 tablespoon Canna Cream provides about 10 mg THC if you have used the Recommended Carrier Amounts table (page 9).

STORAGE: Canna Cream will keep for up to 3 days, tightly covered, in the refrigerator.

1. Bring about 2 inches of water to a boil in the bottom of a double boiler over medium-high heat. Reduce the heat to keep the water simmering.

2. Meanwhile, combine the cream and Cannabis in the top of the double boiler. Place it over the bottom pot, checking to ensure that the simmering water does not touch the bottom of the pot on the top (see Recipe Notes below).

3. Cook the cream, stirring frequently for 30 minutes. Remove the pot from the heat and set it aside to cool.

4. Line a fine-mesh strainer with 1 or 2 layers of cheesecloth or a paper coffee filter. Set the strainer over a 2-cup measuring cup and pour the infused cream from the top of the double boiler through the strainer into the measuring cup. Be patient and let the cream drip through without squeezing or pressing on the filter (see Recipe Note, page 13). Discard the solids, being careful that children or pets cannot access them.

Recipe Notes

- You can make this recipe without a standard double boiler if you have a small heatproof bowl with a lip or a smaller pot that will fit over a larger pot. Bring about 2 inches of water to a boil in the bottom pot and lower the temperature to keep the water simmering. Set the top bowl or pot over the simmering water and test to be sure that the water does not touch the bottom of the top bowl or pot. The steam from the simmering water gently cooks the cream without causing it to curdle or separate. Check to be sure that the water in the bottom pan does not boil away during the 30 minutes of infusing the cream.

- For a vegan infused "cream," substitute high-fat coconut cream or a high-fat (more than 4 grams fat per serving) almond or hemp milk. Note that, of the three, only the coconut cream will whip satisfactorily.

Canna Whipped Cream

->>>>

Makes: 1 cup

¾ cup heavy cream
(36% butterfat)

2 tablespoons Canna Cream
(page 21)

1 teaspoon pure vanilla
extract

¼ cup confectioners' sugar

---

1 serving = 3 tablespoons

DOSE: 3 tablespoons Canna
Whipped Cream provide
about 5 mg THC if you have
used the Recommended
Carrier Amounts table
(page 9).

STORAGE: Canna Whipped
Cream will keep overnight
or up to 1 day, tightly
covered, in the refrigerator.

— Combine the heavy cream, Canna Cream, and vanilla in a large,
deep bowl. Slowly add the sugar while whisking or beating the
cream with an electric beater until stiff peaks form.

Unless otherwise stated in the ingredients list, when milk is called for, you
can use either full- or low-fat dairy milk or a nondairy alternative, such as
almond or rice milk. Most nondairy milk is available in a nonflavored and
unsweetened form. Let your personal taste dictate which style to use.

CANNABIS-INFUSED HONEY

Honey has antibacterial and anti-inflammatory properties, so it makes a good carrier for Cannabis and other medicinal herbs. I use Canna Honey in many sweet recipes in this book, and you can substitute it in your own recipes. Here's how:

- Always use the Recommended Carrier Amounts table (page 9) to determine the amount of honey to infuse for the amount of THC in your strain to ensure a 5 mg THC dose for every teaspoon of honey (see Caution, page 24).

- Make sure the recipe yields 12 servings; you can then substitute ¼ cup Canna Honey for regular honey. If the recipe calls for more than ¼ cup honey, make up the difference by using non-Cannabis-infused honey.

Canna Honey

Liquid honey (see Recommended Carrier Amounts table, page 9 to determine quantity)

¼ ounce (7 grams) powdered, activated Cannabis flower (page 8; see Recipe Notes below)

---

1 serving = 1 teaspoon

DOSE: 1 teaspoon Canna Honey provides about 6 or 7 mg THC if you have used the Recommended Carrier Amounts table (page 9) (see Caution at right).

STORAGE: Infused honey will keep in an airtight container at room temperature for 6 to 12 months.

---

1. Line the bottom of a small (4- to 8-cup) slow cooker with a folded tea towel. Add enough water to fill the crock insert halfway. Turn the heat to low (see Recipe Notes below).

2. Pour the honey into a resealable Mason jar, leaving 1 or 2 inches of headspace. Stir in the powdered Cannabis. Seal the jar and place it on the towel in the water in the slow cooker. Add more hot water, if necessary, to bring the water level to within 2 inches of the top of the sealed jar.

3. Cover the slow cooker with the lid and let it warm on LOW for 4 hours, using oven mitts to swirl the jar every hour. Unplug the slow cooker and set it aside, covered with the lid, for 1 hour or until the jar is cool enough to handle.

4. Dry and label the jar, and store the Canna Honey at room temperature, out of the reach of children.

CAUTION: You may notice that because the Cannabis isn't strained out, honey made with powdered Cannabis may be higher in THC than oils that have the still-viable flower material removed. This explains why I've noted that 1 teaspoon unfiltered Canna Honey provides more than 5 mg THC, even though you have used the recommended amount of carrier.

Recipe Notes

- Lining the bottom of the slow cooker with a folded tea towel before heating the water in step 1 keeps the honey and the Cannabis from scorching.

- Because it's too messy to strain infused honey (as we do infused fats), I use powdered Cannabis (and power herbs) which easily dissolves into the honey. Using powdered instead of coarsely chopped Cannabis yields a greenish-colored honey. Use a dedicated spice grinder (a coffee grinder only used for herbs and spices) to powder activated (decarboxylated) Cannabis.

>>>> Canna Healing Honey

For extra healing power, add one or two of the healing herbs recommended in Appendix B (page 186). For example, for pain you can add ground willow bark, and for insomnia try ground valerian or chamomile.

Liquid honey (see Recommended Carrier Amounts table, page 9, to determine quantity)

¼ ounce (7 grams) powdered, activated Cannabis flower (page 8; see also Recipe Notes, page 24)

1 tablespoon ground herb of your choice (see Appendix B, page 186)

2 tablespoons lecithin, optional

---

1 serving = 1 teaspoon

DOSE: 1 teaspoon Canna Healing Honey provides about 6 or 7 mg THC (see Caution, page 24) if you have used the Recommended Carrier Amounts table (page 9).

STORAGE: Canna Healing Honey will keep at room temperature for 6 to 12 months.

---

1. Line the bottom of a small (4- to 8-cup) slow cooker with a folded tea towel. Add enough water to fill the crock halfway. Turn the heat to low (see Recipe Notes opposite).

2. Pour the honey into a Mason jar, leaving 1 or 2 inches of headspace. Stir in the powdered Cannabis, ground herb, and lecithin (if using). Seal the jar and place it on the towel in the water in the slow cooker. Add more hot water, if necessary, to bring the water level to within 2 inches of the top of the sealed jar.

3. Cover the slow cooker with the lid and let warm on LOW for 4 hours, using oven mitts to swirl the jar every hour. Unplug the slow cooker and set it aside, covered with the lid, for 1 hour or until the jar is cool enough to handle.

4. Dry and label the jar, and store the Canna Healing Honey at room temperature, out of the reach of children.

CANNABIS-INFUSED COMPOUND BUTTERS

Compound butters add an intense flavor to cooked vegetables, grilled or steamed fish, meat, pasta, rice, soups, and cooked cereals. Keep them at room temperature to spread on toast or bread. If you like the taste and texture of the spent Cannabis herb (left over from infusing ghee or coconut oil; see "Waste Not," page 14), substitute one-quarter of it for the Canna Ghee or Canna Coco Oil called for in the recipe.

I call the following recipes Canna "butters," however, you can use Canna Coco Oil (page 13), in place of the unsalted butter for a vegan "butter." Storing Canna Coco Oil at just below 76°F (24°C) will ensure that it is solid yet soft enough to scoop into a measuring cup.

>>> Canna Herb Butter

Makes: about 1 cup

¼ cup Canna Ghee (page 16) or Canna Coco Oil (page 13)

½ cup unsalted butter, at room temperature, or extra-virgin coconut oil (see Cannabis-Infused Compound Butters, above)

¼ cup chopped fresh herbs (chives, thyme, oregano, marjoram, cilantro, parsley)

1 clove garlic, minced

2 teaspoons lemon zest

1. Combine Canna Ghee, butter, herbs, garlic, and lemon zest in a food processor. Process for 30 seconds or until well mixed.

2. Transfer the butter to a jar. Seal, label, and store the jar in the refrigerator, out of the reach of children.

---

1 serving = 1 tablespoon

DOSE: 1 tablespoon Canna Herb Butter provides about 4 mg THC if you have used the Recommended Carrier Amounts table (page 9) to make the Canna Ghee.

STORAGE: Canna Herb Butter will keep in an airtight container in the refrigerator for up to 2 weeks.

TO FREEZE: Measure tablespoon-size portions onto a parchment-lined, rimmed baking sheet and freeze for about 1 hour or until solid. Transfer to a resealable bag or freezer container, seal, label, and freeze. Use within 6 months.

>>>> Ayurvedic Canna Butter

Ayurveda is an ancient health system that was developed in India to holistically treat the mind-body-spirit. It has survived over 3,000 years. While there are spices that benefit specific body types (*doshas*), the following assist everyone in digestion and help lower inflammation. Use the following ground (powdered) spices in any combination for this butter recipe:

Cumin – Coriander seeds – Fennel seeds – Mustard seeds

Fenugreek – Turmeric – Ginger *(exception: use freshly grated)*

¼ cup Canna Ghee (page 16) or Canna Coco Oil (page 13)

½ cup unsalted butter, at room temperature, or extra-virgin coconut oil (see Cannabis-Infused Compound Butters, opposite)

¼ cup chopped fresh herbs (chives, thyme, oregano, marjoram, cilantro, parsley)

1 clove garlic, minced

1 tablespoon ground Ayurvedic spice or combination of your choice (see list above)

2 teaspoons lemon zest

1. Combine Canna Ghee, butter, herbs, garlic, spice, and lemon zest in a food processor. Process for 30 seconds or until well combined.

2. Transfer the butter to a jar. Seal and label the jar, and store it in the refrigerator, out of the reach of children.

1 serving = 1 tablespoon

DOSE: 1 tablespoon Ayurvedic Canna Butter provides about 4 mg THC if you have used the Recommended Carrier Amounts table (page 9) to make the Canna Ghee.

STORAGE: Ayurvedic Canna Butter will keep in an airtight container in the refrigerator for up to 3 weeks.

TO FREEZE: Measure tablespoon-size portions onto a parchment-lined, rimmed baking sheet and freeze for about 1 hour or until solid. Transfer to a resealable bag or freezer container, seal, label, and freeze. Use within 6 months.

>>> Canna Miso Butter

¼ cup Canna Ghee (page 16) or Canna Coco Oil (page 13)

½ cup unsalted butter, at room temperature, or extra-virgin coconut oil (see Cannabis-Infused Compound Butters, page 26)

¼ cup chopped fresh herbs (chives, thyme, oregano, marjoram, cilantro, parsley)

¼ cup miso (see Recipe Note at right)

2 teaspoons lemon zest

---

1 serving = 1 tablespoon

DOSE: 1 tablespoon Canna Miso Butter provides about 4 mg THC if you have used the Recommended Carrier Amounts table (page 9) to make the Canna Ghee.

STORAGE: Canna Miso Butter will keep in the refrigerator for up to 3 weeks.

TO FREEZE: Measure tablespoon-size portions onto a parchment-lined, rimmed baking sheet and freeze for about 1 hour or until solid. Transfer to a resealable bag or container, seal, and label. Keep in the freezer and use within 6 months.

1. Combine Canna Ghee, butter, herbs, miso, and lemon zest in a food processor. Process for 30 seconds or until well mixed.

2. Transfer to a jar, seal, label, and store in the refrigerator, out of the reach of children.

Recipe Note

- Miso is a high-protein, aged or fermented seasoning, made from soybeans, cultured grain, salt, and water. It adds a salty, umami flavor to recipes. You can use red, white, or brown miso in this recipe.

CANNABIS-INFUSED NUT BUTTERS

Due to their high fat content, nut butters make a very good medium for infusing Cannabis. Any nut butter—cashew, almond, walnut, sesame (tahini), peanut, pumpkin, etc.—may be used to make a healing Cannabis-infused nut butter. Make your own nut butter following the recipe for Homemade Canna Nut Butter (page 30) or Spiced Canna Nut Butter (page 31) or purchase your favorite unsweetened nut butter to use in the easy Canna Nut Butter recipe (below).

Over time, the oil in Homemade Canna Nut Butter may separate and float to the top. This is because no emulsifiers are used in the recipe. You can scrape the nut butter and the separated oil into a food processor and blend it, or use a knife to cut through the paste at the bottom and mix the oil into it by hand.

Use Cannabis-infused nut butters with cooked or roasted vegetables or pasta, or add them to tomato-based condiments, such as Canna Churri (page 45), Peanut Sauce (page 123), or Canna Salsa (page 113).

NOTE: Do not use Canna Nut Butter together with Canna Oil (page 15) in the same recipe. If you do, be aware that the amount of THC in every dose will double.

>>>> Canna Nut Butter

Cannabis-Infused Nut Butter, using commercial nut butter

Makes: 1¼ cups

1 cup regular nut butter of your choice (not Cannabis-infused)

¼ cup Canna Coco Oil (page 13) or Canna Oil (page 15)

2 tablespoons liquid honey, optional

1. Combine the nut butter, Canna Coco Oil, and honey (if using) in a food processor and process for 30 seconds to 1 minute or until smooth.

2. Transfer the Canna Nut Butter to a jar, seal, and label. Store at room temperature or in the refrigerator, out of the reach of children.

1 serving = 2 tablespoons

DOSE: 2 tablespoons Canna Nut Butter provides about 5 mg THC if you have used the Recommended Carrier Amounts table (page 9) to make the Canna Coco Oil.

STORAGE: Canna Nut Butter will keep in the refrigerator for up to 3 weeks.

>>>> Homemade Canna Nut Butter

Homemade Cannabis-Infused Nut Butter

Makes: about 1 cup

2 cups roasted shelled nuts (see Recipe Notes below)

2 tablespoons Canna Coco Oil (page 13) or Canna Oil (page 15)

2 tablespoons liquid honey, optional

¼ to ½ teaspoon sea salt, or to taste (see Recipe Notes below)

---

1 serving = 2 tablespoons

DOSE: **2 tablespoons Homemade Canna Nut Butter provides about 4 mg THC if you have used the Recommended Carrier Amounts table (page 9) to make the Canna Coco Oil.**

STORAGE: **Homemade Canna Nut Butter will keep in the refrigerator for up to 3 weeks.**

---

1. Combine the nuts, Canna Coco Oil, honey (if using), and salt in a food processor and process for 2 to 3 minutes. Stop and scrape the sides, using a rubber spatula. Replace the lid and process for 10 to 15 minutes, stopping to scrape the sides occasionally, until the desired consistency is reached.

2. Transfer the nut butter to a jar, seal, and label. Store at room temperature or in the refrigerator, out of the reach of children.

Recipe Notes

- Use any nut, such as almonds, cashews, pistachios, or a combination of nuts, and sunflower or pumpkin seeds. I like to roast the nuts before making nut butter because it helps release their oils and intensifies their flavor. To roast nuts, spread them in a single layer on a rimmed baking sheet and roast at 350°F for 5 to 10 minutes, stirring after 5 minutes, until lightly colored.

- If you use salted nuts, taste and adjust the amount of salt (if any) that you add.

- Store Homemade Canna Nut Butters in the refrigerator because, unlike commercial nut butter, they do not contain preservatives. Bring to room temperature before using.

Spiced Canna Nut Butter

Cannabis-Infused Nut Butter with Spices

Makes: about 1 cup

1 cup homemade or store-bought regular nut butter (not Cannabis-infused)

2 tablespoons Canna Nut Butter (page 29) or Homemade Canna Nut Butter (page 30)

2 tablespoons liquid honey, optional

1 tablespoon ground cinnamon or an Ayurvedic spice (page 27) or a combination of your choice (see Recipe Notes below)

---

1 serving = 2 tablespoons

DOSE: 2 tablespoons Spiced Canna Nut Butter provides about 4 mg THC if you have used the Recommended Carrier Amounts table (page 9) to make the Canna Nut Butter.

STORAGE: Spiced Canna Nut Butter will keep in the refrigerator for up to 3 weeks.

---

1. Combine regular nut butter, Canna Nut Butter, honey (if using), and spice in a food processor and process for 30 seconds to 1 minute or until well mixed.

2. Transfer to a jar, seal, and label. Store at room temperature or in the refrigerator, out of the reach of children.

Recipe Notes

- You can use any spice or combination of spices in this recipe, including any of the Cannabis-infused spice pastes (beginning on page 40).

- If you choose to use a Cannabis-infused spice paste, add 1 tablespoon of infused spice paste and 1 tablespoon of the Canna Nut Butter or Homemade Canna Nut Butter to keep the amount of THC per serving to 4 mg.

CANNABIS-INFUSED TINCTURES

Herbalists and holistic healers follow an age-old tradition of preserving the active healing components in herbs by immersing the herbs in alcohol and warming the mixture in a sunny place. The alcohol extracts medicinal constituents from the herbs and preserves them at the same time. For your own tinctures, you can use raw or activated Cannabis or a mixture of Cannabis and other healing power herbs (see Appendix B, page 186).

Don't dismiss tinctures as strictly medicine. You can add 1 teaspoon of Cannabis-infused tincture to smoothies, juices, teas, hot chocolate drinks, and other hot or cold, nonalcoholic drinks. Tinctures come in handy if you want to add Cannabis to only one serving of soup, stew, or another dish at the table and don't want to add a Cannabis-infused fat.

For children, or adults who wish to avoid alcohol, safe alternatives include glycerine, apple cider vinegar, or soft apple cider. Glycerine has the added benefit of being sweet, so it also appeals to children, but I'm not convinced that it is as effective at drawing out the cannabinoids in Cannabis as are fats and alcohol. Keep in mind that THC is *not* to be given to children and young people under the age of 25, so only use raw THCA in tinctures for this age group.

The two Cannabis tincture recipes that follow can be stacked with a power herb. To determine the most effective healing herbs, if you are treating a condition, check the list of herbs in Appendix B, page 186. Choose one, possibly two, herbs from those listed for a condition and combine them with raw or activated Cannabis. Both recipes call for dried herbs, but if you have them, use twice the amount of fresh chopped herbs.

➤ >>> Canna Tincture (alcohol)

¼ ounce (7 grams) roughly chopped raw or activated dried Cannabis (page 8)

¼ cup ground dried herbs or ½ cup chopped fresh herbs, optional (see Cannabis-Infused Tinctures opposite)

40% or 45% alcohol (see Recipe Notes below; see Recommended Carrier Amounts table, page 9 to determine quantity)

---

1 serving = 1 teaspoon

DOSE: 1 teaspoon Canna Tincture provides about 5 mg THC if you have used the Recommended Carrier Amounts table (page 9).

STORAGE: Alcohol and vinegar tinctures will keep for years at a cool room temperature or in the refrigerator.

---

1. Combine Cannabis and herbs (if using) in a 2-cup (or larger) jar. Add alcohol, leaving a ½-inch headspace and cover with a lid. Shake well. Label and store the tincture in a dark cupboard, out of the reach of children, for 1 to 2 months, shaking once a day or every few days, whenever you remember. You can strain the tincture immediately or leave it indefinitely until you're ready to use it.

2. *To strain the tincture:* Line a fine-mesh strainer with a basket-style paper coffee filter or a double layer of cheesecloth. Set the strainer over a 2-cup measuring cup and pour the infused alcohol from the jar through the strainer into the measuring cup. Be patient and let the tincture drip through without squeezing or pressing on the filter (see Recipe Note, page 13). Reserve the solids for another use (see Recipe Notes below) or discard them.

3. Transfer the tincture to a 2-cup jar or pour it into small, dark dropper bottles. Seal, label, and store the tincture in a cool, dark place, out of the reach of children.

Recipe Notes

- For tinctures, I use 80 to 90 proof (40%–45%) vodka, but rum or brandy will also work, as long as they are a high proof (United States term) or at least 40 percent alcohol (Canadian term). For an alcohol-free version, substitute an equal quantity of apple cider vinegar or soft apple cider, but you will get more potent results using alcohol. Add 1 teaspoon of tincture to juices, smoothies, or teas. Or simply take a dose (1 teaspoon) of Canna Tincture directly under the tongue.

- If you want to reserve the remaining plant material after straining (and I recommend that you do because it's still potent) for use in another recipe, such as Calming Latte (page 167) or Canna-Cocoa (page 174), transfer it to a jar, seal, label, and store in a cool, dark cupboard, out of the reach of children. Use it within 1 month.

¼ ounce (7 grams) roughly chopped raw or activated dried Cannabis (page 8)

¼ cup ground dried herbs or ½ cup chopped fresh herbs, optional (see Cannabis-Infused Tinctures, page 32)

Organic vegetable glycerine (see Recipe Notes opposite; also see the Recommended Carrier Amounts table, page 9, to determine quantity)

Distilled water: Use 1 part water to every 3 parts glycerine (see Recipe Notes opposite)

---

1 serving = 1 teaspoon

DOSE: 1 teaspoon Canna Tincture provides about 5 mg THC if you have used the Recommended Carrier Amounts table (page 9).

STORAGE: Glycerine tinctures will keep for up to 2 years in the refrigerator.

---

1. Combine Cannabis and herbs (if using) in a 2- to 6-cup jar (see Recipe Notes to determine the size of jar). Seal and shake well to mix.

2. In a bowl or measuring cup, combine glycerine and water and mix well.

3. Pour the glycerine mixture into the jar with the Cannabis-herb mixture to about the halfway point. Seal and shake to mix the ingredients.

4. Add the remaining glycerine mixture to the jar, leaving a ½- to 1-inch headspace. Seal, label, and shake well. Set aside in the refrigerator for about 2 months, shaking it once a day or every few days, whenever you remember.

5. Set a fine-mesh strainer over a 2- to 6-cup measuring cup and pour the infused glycerine from the jar through the strainer into the measuring cup. Be patient and let the tincture drip through without squeezing or pressing on the filter (see Recipe Note, page 13). Reserve solids for another use (see "Waste Not," page 14) or discard them.

6. Transfer the tincture to one, two, or three 2-cup jars, or pour it into small, dark dropper bottles. Seal, label, and store in the refrigerator out of the reach of children.

Recipe Notes

- For this tincture, you mix vegetable glycerine with distilled water. Once you determine the amount of carrier to use for the percentage of THC in your strain, you will need to calculate what one-quarter of that total amount is for the water portion. The quarter amount of water and three quarters glycerine make up the total amount of carrier to use for the percentage of THC in your strain.

- Once you determine the amount of carrier to use for the percentage of THC in your strain (from the Recommended Carrier Amounts table on page 9), you can determine the size of jar to use for the tincture.

- If you want to reserve the remaining plant material (and I recommend that you do because it's still potent) for use in another recipe, such as Calming Latte (page 167) or Canna-Cocoa (page 174), transfer it to a jar, then seal, label, and store in a cool, dark cupboard, out of the reach of children. Use within 1 month.

CANNABIS-INFUSED SIMPLE SYRUP

In the Middle Ages, without the benefit of refrigeration, monks, wise women, and other herbalists relied on the preserving qualities of salt, vinegar, alcohol, and sugar to extract and preserve the healing benefits of the plants they grew for symptom relief. Simple syrup made from water, sugar, and chopped fresh or dried herbs was called a "rob," and one of the earliest was Elderberry Rob, made by simmering five pounds of ripe, crushed elderberries with one pound of sugar until the juice was as thick as honey. Fresh juice or herbal teas keep for a couple of days, at the most, while the same liquids, when simmered with sugar, will keep without refrigeration for a season or more.

Note that I do not use enough sugar in my simple syrup recipes to make them stable at room temperature, so I recommend storing them in the refrigerator.

Cannabis-infused syrup can be added to hot or iced tea or coffee, used in place of honey in recipes, drizzled over ice cream, or used to make a fruit trifle dessert. Try making these stunningly beautiful Cannabis-infused syrups and use them whenever you wish to spike mocktails or enjoy as an after-dinner sip.

Lemon-Ginger Simple Syrup

2 cups water

2 cups superfine (caster) sugar

2 tablespoons grated fresh ginger

1 tablespoon grated lemon zest

Juice of 1 or 2 lemons

Canna Honey (page 24; see Recipe Notes below)

---

1 serving = see Recipe Notes below

DOSE: See Recipe Notes below. One teaspoon Canna Honey provides about 5 mg THC if you have used the Recommended Carrier Amounts table (page 9).

1. Bring the water to a boil in a large saucepan over medium-high heat. Stir in the sugar and bring the mixture to a simmer, stirring frequently. Add the ginger, lemon zest, and juice from 1 lemon and bring the mixture back to a simmer. Turn the heat off, cover the pan with a lid, and let it sit on the burner until it is cool, about 1 hour. Taste the syrup and add more lemon juice if desired.

2. Set a fine-mesh strainer over a 3-cup measuring cup. Line the strainer with cheesecloth and pour the syrup through the strainer into the measuring cup. Let the syrup drip through without squeezing or pressing on the solids. Discard the solids.

3. Decide how much syrup you want to use as a serving. Check the Recipe Notes below for the amount of Canna Honey to add, and stir it into the syrup.

4. Using a funnel, pour the syrup into one 2-cup jar or several smaller jars. Cap and label the jar(s), clearly marking the serving size, and store in the refrigerator out of the reach of children.

Recipe Notes

• With syrup, in order to keep dosage at about 5 mg, you need to decide how much you will use in a single serving. To add to a drink, 1 tablespoon syrup is appropriate, but to use syrup for dessert, ¼ cup might be the serving size. Since this recipe makes 2 cups of syrup, here are the amounts of Canna Honey to add for a small (1 tablespoon) or a larger (¼-cup) serving:

  – 1 tablespoon serving size, add ¾ cup Canna Honey
  – ¼ cup serving size, add a scant 3 tablespoons Canna Honey

Raspberry-Thyme Simple Syrup

Makes: 2 cups

2 cups water

2 cups superfine (caster) sugar

1 cup raspberries, fresh or frozen

1 handful (about 10) fresh thyme sprigs

1 tablespoon freshly squeezed lemon juice

Canna Honey (page 24; see Recipe Notes below)

Sea salt, to taste

---

1 serving = see Recipe Notes below

DOSE: 1 teaspoon Canna Honey provides about 5 mg THC if you have used the Recommended Carrier Amounts table (page 9).

---

1. Bring the water to a boil in a large saucepan over medium-high heat. Stir in the sugar and bring the water to a simmer, stirring frequently. Add the raspberries, thyme, and lemon juice to the pan and bring the mixture back to a simmer, stirring frequently for about 10 minutes or until the raspberries collapse. Turn off the heat, cover the pan with a lid, and let the pan sit on the stove until it's partially cool, about 30 minutes. Taste the syrup mixture and add a pinch of salt if desired.

2. Set a fine-mesh strainer over a 3-cup measuring cup. Line the strainer with cheesecloth and pour the syrup through the strainer into the measuring cup. Let the syrup drip through without squeezing or pressing on the solids. Discard the solids or freeze them in ¼-cup containers and add them to smoothie drinks.

3. Decide how much syrup you want to use as a serving. Check the Recipe Notes below for the amount of Canna Honey to add and stir it into the syrup.

4. Using a funnel, pour the syrup into one 2-cup jar or several smaller jars. Cap and label the jar(s), clearly marking serving size, and store them in the refrigerator out of the reach of children.

Recipe Notes

- For syrup, to keep dosage at about 5 mg, you need to decide how much you will use in a single serving. To add to a drink, 1 tablespoon is appropriate, but to use syrup for a dessert, ¼ cup could be the serving size. Since this recipe makes 2 cups of syrup, here are the amounts of Canna Honey to add for a small (1 tablespoon) or a larger (¼-cup) serving:

   – 1 tablespoon serving size, add ¾ cup Canna Honey
   – ¼ cup serving size, add a scant 3 tablespoons Canna Honey

Matcha-Rosemary Simple Syrup

2 cups water

2 tablespoons Anti-Inflammatory Matcha Tea Blend (page 69; see Recipe Notes below)

2 cups superfine (caster) sugar

Canna Honey (page 24; see Recipe Notes below)

3 sprigs (2 inches each) fresh rosemary

---

1 serving = see Recipe Notes below

DOSE: 1 teaspoon Canna Honey provides about 5 mg THC if you have used the Recommended Carrier Amounts table (page 9).

---

1. Bring the water to a boil in a kettle and pour it into a 2-cup measure. Add the tea blend to a large saucepan and pour in the 2 cups of boiled water. Cover the pan and set it aside to let the tea steep for 12 minutes.

2. Heat the liquid in the saucepan over medium-high heat. Stir in the sugar and bring the mixture to a simmer, stirring frequently. Turn off the heat, cover the pan with a lid, and let the pan sit on the stove until it is partially cool, about 30 minutes.

3. Set a fine-mesh strainer over a 3-cup measuring cup. Line the strainer with cheesecloth and pour the syrup through the strainer into the measuring cup. Let the syrup drip through without squeezing or pressing on the solids. Discard the solids.

4. Decide how much syrup you want to use as a serving. Check the Recipe Notes below for the amount of Canna Honey to add, and stir it into the syrup.

5. Pack the rosemary sprigs into a 2-cup jar or pack 1 sprig in each of 3 smaller jars. Using a funnel, pour the syrup into the jar(s). Cap and label the jar(s), clearly marking serving size, and store in the refrigerator out of the reach of children.

Recipe Notes

- Anti-Inflammatory Matcha Tea Blend is perfect for this simple syrup, but if you haven't made the blend, you can use 1 tablespoon matcha tea powder and 1 tablespoon ground sage.

- With syrup, in order to keep dosage at about 5 mg, you need to decide how much you will use in a single serving. To add to a drink, 1 tablespoon is appropriate, but to use syrup for a dessert, ¼ cup might be the serving size. Since the recipe makes 2 cups of syrup, here are the amounts of Canna Honey to add for a small (1 tablespoon) or a larger (¼-cup) serving:

  – 1 tablespoon serving size, add ¾ cup Canna Honey
  – ¼ cup serving size, add a scant 3 tablespoons Canna Honey

CANNABIS-INFUSED SPICE PASTES

Spice pastes add flavor to both savory and sweet recipes. They may contain fruit, vegetables, or oil, as well as Cannabis-infused fats, spices, and herbs. If you have a spice paste at your disposal, you will find it easy to spike your own food with 1 tablespoon of Cannabis-concentrated flavor and pass it along to any other adults at the table who wish to add Cannabis to their food.

Toss 1 tablespoon of any of the four pastes that follow with a serving of cooked pasta, rice, or noodles, or add it to juice, smoothie drinks, herbal tea, or soup. Try mixing a tablespoon with cooked vegetables or toasted nuts, or spread it on crackers, cookies, or bread for an instant taste sensation.

Canna Curry Spice Paste

Canna Curry Spice Paste

Makes: 1 cup

2 tablespoons coriander seeds

5 teaspoons fenugreek seeds

1 tablespoon cumin seeds

1 tablespoon fennel seeds

3 cloves garlic, peeled and quartered

2 dried cayenne chile peppers, roughly chopped

1 tablespoon freshly grated, peeled ginger

¼ cup Canna Oil (page 15) or Canna Coco Oil (page 13)

1 tablespoon ground turmeric

2 teaspoons ground cinnamon

1 teaspoon sea salt

2 tablespoons extra-virgin olive oil or liquid honey (for a slightly sweet paste)

1. Combine the coriander, fenugreek, cumin, and fennel seeds in a small, dry skillet over medium-high heat. Toast the seeds, stirring them constantly, for 1 minute or until the smaller seeds begin to pop. Do not allow the seeds to burn. Transfer the seeds to a plate and set aside to cool.

2. Grind the seeds to a coarse or fine powder using a mortar and pestle or a spice grinder. Set them aside.

3. Process the garlic, peppers, and ginger in a food processor for 30 seconds or until combined. Add the Canna Oil, turmeric, cinnamon, salt, and ground seeds. Process for 30 seconds or until blended into a smooth paste. Drizzle olive oil on top and process for 20 seconds more, or until all the ingredients are well mixed into the paste.

4. Transfer the paste to a jar, and then seal and label it. Store the paste in the refrigerator, out of the reach of children.

1 serving = 1 tablespoon

DOSE: 1 tablespoon Canna Curry Spice Paste provides about 4 mg THC if you have used the Recommended Carrier Amounts table (page 9) to make the Canna Oil.

STORAGE: Canna Curry Spice Paste will keep in an airtight container in the refrigerator for up to 2 weeks.

TO FREEZE: Drop tablespoon-size portions of Canna Curry Spice Paste onto a parchment-lined rimmed baking sheet. Freeze for 1 hour or until solid. Transfer to a resealable bag or container, seal, label, and freeze for up to 6 months.

>>>> Canna Mediterranean Herb Paste

Makes: ¼ cup

5 cloves garlic, quartered

¼ cup fresh thyme leaves

3 tablespoons chopped fresh sage

1 tablespoon chopped fresh rosemary

2 teaspoons chopped fresh French tarragon

2 teaspoons prepared Dijon mustard

½ teaspoon sea salt

¼ cup Canna Oil (page 15) or Canna Coco Oil (page 13)

1 tablespoon white wine vinegar

1. Combine the garlic, thyme, sage, rosemary, tarragon, mustard, and salt in a food processor. Pulse for 30 seconds or until the mixture is finely chopped.

2. Add 2 tablespoons of Canna Oil and process until combined. Add the vinegar and the remaining Canna Oil and process until blended.

3. Transfer the paste to a jar. Seal and label the jar, and store it in the refrigerator, out of the reach of children.

---

1 serving = 1 tablespoon

DOSE: 1 tablespoon Canna Mediterranean Herb Paste provides about 5 mg THC if you have used the Recommended Carrier Amounts table (page 9) to make the Canna Oil.

STORAGE: Canna Mediterranean Herb Paste will keep in the refrigerator for up to 2 weeks.

TO FREEZE: Drop tablespoon-size portions onto a parchment-lined rimmed baking sheet. Freeze for about 1 hour or until solid. Transfer to a resealable bag or container, seal, label, and freeze for up to 6 months.

Sweet Canna Thai Spice Paste

Makes: 1 cup

¼ cup Canna Oil (page 15) or Canna Coco Oil (page 13)

2 tablespoons liquid honey

4 cloves garlic, quartered

3 tablespoons ground cinnamon

2 tablespoons ground turmeric

1 tablespoon hot mustard powder

1 tablespoon freshly grated, peeled ginger

2 teaspoons ground black pepper

1 teaspoon hot chile powder, or to taste

2 tablespoons apple cider vinegar

1. Combine Canna Oil, honey, and garlic in a food processor and process for 30 seconds or until garlic is chopped and the ingredients are well blended.

2. Add the cinnamon, turmeric, mustard powder, ginger, black pepper, and chile powder. Process for 30 seconds or until well incorporated. With the motor running, add just enough vinegar through the feed tube to make a thick paste.

3. Transfer the paste to a jar. Seal and label the jar, and store it in the refrigerator, out of the reach of children.

---

1 serving = 1 tablespoon

DOSE: 1 tablespoon Sweet Canna Thai Spice Paste provides about 4 mg THC if you have used the Recommended Carrier Amounts table (page 9) to make the Canna Oil.

STORAGE: Sweet Canna Thai Spice Paste will keep in an airtight container in the refrigerator for up to 2 weeks.

TO FREEZE: Drop tablespoon-size portions of Sweet Canna Thai Spice Paste onto a parchment-lined rimmed baking sheet. Freeze for about 1 hour or until solid. Transfer to a resealable bag or container, seal, label, and freeze for up to 6 months.

>>>> Red-Hot Canna Curry Paste

Makes: about 1 cup

½ cup dried cayenne peppers

¼ cup Canna Oil (page 15) or Canna Coco Oil (page 13)

3 cloves garlic, quartered

2 stalks lemongrass, tough outer leaves and woody base removed, sliced

1 roasted red pepper

1 tablespoon ground turmeric

1 (1-inch) piece fresh or candied ginger, finely chopped

1 tablespoon white wine vinegar

½ teaspoon sea salt

1. Place the cayenne peppers in a small bowl. Cover the peppers with just-boiled water and set them aside for 20 minutes to soak and soften. Drain the peppers, reserving a small amount of the soaking liquid and discarding the rest. Transfer the peppers to a blender or a food processor.

2. Add the Canna Oil, garlic, lemongrass, roasted pepper, turmeric, ginger, vinegar, and salt to the cayenne peppers. Pulse for 30 seconds or until blended. The mixture should be thick and paste-like but not dry. If it's too dry, add the reserved liquid, 1 tablespoon at a time, and pulse until the desired consistency is reached.

3. Transfer the paste to a jar. Seal and label the jar, and store it in the refrigerator, out of the reach of children.

1 serving = 1 tablespoon

DOSE: 1 tablespoon Red-Hot Canna Curry Paste provides about 4 mg THC if you have used the Recommended Carrier Amounts table (page 9) to make the Canna Oil.

STORAGE: Red-Hot Canna Curry Paste will keep in the refrigerator for up to 2 weeks.

TO FREEZE: Drop tablespoon-size portions onto a parchment-lined rimmed baking sheet. Freeze for about 1 hour or until solid. Transfer to a resealable bag or container, seal, label, and freeze for up to 6 months.

CANNABIS-INFUSED SPREADS

When Cannabis is added to spreads or dips, you need to be mindful of the amount you use. Always measure the serving amount, and only exceed it when you are experienced enough to know what the perfect amount of THC is for you (see "Your First Cannabis Edibles Test," page 18). The exception to this rule is when raw Cannabis, which does not pack a psychedelic punch, is used in a recipe such as Cannabis Leaf Pesto (page 49). You can use raw Cannabis in any quantity you like in a recipe or as an addition to a sandwich or a main dish.

But if you know that 1 tablespoon of Canna Churri or Canna Mayo is not enough to make a sandwich or to mix into a salad, combine one serving per person of the Canna version with as much as you need of a non-Cannabis mayonnaise. This will keep the dose at 5 mg THC.

>>>> Canna Churri

Makes: about 1 cup

3 cloves garlic, minced

2 tablespoons red wine vinegar

2 teaspoons prepared Dijon mustard

2 tablespoons lightly packed brown sugar

½ teaspoon sea salt

¼ cup Canna Oil (page 15) or Canna Coco Oil (page 13)

2 tomatoes, coarsely chopped

1 cup finely chopped fresh parsley

½ cup coarsely chopped fresh Cannabis leaves, optional

3 tablespoons chopped fresh oregano

1 tablespoon chopped fresh rosemary

1. Combine the garlic, vinegar, mustard, sugar, and salt in a medium bowl. Stir to mix well.

2. Drizzle the Canna Oil over the garlic mixture in the bowl, and whisk it with a fork to combine all the ingredients.

3. Add the tomatoes, parsley, Cannabis leaves (if using), oregano, and rosemary to the bowl and toss to mix well.

4. Transfer the Canna Churri to a jar. Seal and label the jar, and store it in the refrigerator, out of the reach of children.

1 serving = 1 tablespoon

DOSE: 1 tablespoon Canna Churri provides about 5 mg THC if you have used the Recommended Carrier Amounts table (page 9) to make the Canna Oil.

STORAGE: Canna Churri will keep in the refrigerator for up to 2 weeks.

TO FREEZE: Drop 1 tablespoon-size portions onto a parchment-lined rimmed baking sheet. Freeze for about 1 hour or until solid. Transfer to a resealable bag or container, seal, label, and freeze for up to 6 months.

Easy Canna Mayo

1 cup commercially prepared mayonnaise (see Recipe Note below)

2 tablespoons Canna Oil (page 15)

1 tablespoon freshly squeezed lemon juice

---

1 serving = 2 to 3 tablespoons

DOSE: 2 to 3 tablespoons Easy Canna Mayo provides about 4 to 6 mg THC if you have used the Recommended Carrier Amounts table (page 9) to make the Canna Oil.

STORAGE: Easy Canna Mayo will keep in a covered container in the refrigerator for up to 3 weeks.

— Place the mayonnaise in a small bowl. Slowly whisk in the Canna Oil using a fork or a whisk. Slowly whisk in the lemon juice.

Recipe Note

• For this recipe, I like to use a "real" mayonnaise, not salad spread.

>>> Canna Mayo

Cannabis-Infused Aioli (fresh mayonnaise)

Makes: ¾ cup

1 clove garlic

½ teaspoon sea salt

1 tablespoon Dijon mustard

1 large egg yolk

2 tablespoons Canna Oil
(page 15)

2 tablespoons freshly
squeezed lemon juice

½ cup extra-virgin olive oil

---

1 serving = 2 tablespoons

DOSE: **2 tablespoons Canna Mayo provides about 5 mg THC if you have used the Recommended Carrier Amounts table (page 9) to make the Canna Oil.**

STORAGE: Canna Mayo will keep in the refrigerator for up to 2 days.

---

1. Combine the garlic, salt, and mustard in a blender or a small food processor and process for 20 seconds. Add the egg yolk and process for 10 seconds.

2. With the motor running, slowly drizzle the Canna Oil into the mixture through the feed tube and slowly add the lemon juice. Keep the motor running and very slowly add the olive oil, just until the mixture begins to thicken. Scrape the mayo into a jar. Tightly cover and label the jar, and keep it in the refrigerator.

CAUTION: Be aware that Canna Mayo (not just Cannabis-infused aioli but all fresh mayonnaise) contains raw egg yolk, which can cause digestive upset in some people and should not be given to infants and small children. Always keep Canna Mayo (aioli) in the refrigerator and use within 2 days.

Recipe Notes

- Homemade aioli is much more flavorful than commercially prepared mayonnaise, but always keep aioli in the refrigerator and use it within 2 days (see Caution above).

- Homemade mayonnaise (aioli) thickens when chilled.

- For an easy Canna Mayo with no raw egg yolk, see Easy Canna Mayo opposite.

Cannabis Leaf Pesto

(a raw Cannabis recipe)

2 cloves garlic

1½ cups lightly packed fresh
basil leaves

½ cup coarsely chopped
fresh Cannabis leaves

¾ cup freshly grated
Parmesan cheese

½ cup sunflower seeds

½ teaspoon sea salt

¾ cup extra-virgin
avocado oil

1. Chop the garlic in a food processor or blender. Add the basil and Cannabis and process for 30 seconds. Add the cheese, sunflower seeds, and salt. With the motor running, slowly pour the oil through the feed tube and process until well mixed.

2. Transfer the pesto to a jar. Seal, label, and store the jar in the refrigerator, out of the reach of children.

STORAGE: Cannabis Leaf Pesto will keep, tightly covered, in the refrigerator for up to 2 weeks.

CHAPTER 2

< Morning Beverages and Light Meals >

For people living with chronic pain or inflammation, Cannabis puts the "good" in *Good morning*. Starting your days with smoothies, raw juice, breakfast bars, and grab-and-go foods enriched with Cannabis can help you hit the ground running. Euphemistically referred to as *Wake and Bake*, a mini dose of Cannabis can raise your spirits and help you face whatever work and life might bring.

Keep in mind that when your stomach is empty in the morning, THC is more potent. My advice is to make sure you use a sativa-dominant strain for your morning meal or beverage, because typically it increases creativity, focus, and energy. I also recommend that you look for a sativa strain with equal or higher CBD to no more than 6 percent THC, and take a very low dose (1 to 5 mg THC), because an energized state of mind is the goal, not a high.

Don't overlook your body's need for protein, vitamins, minerals, and some carbohydrates to break your fast, which is why three hearty smoothies kick off the recipes in this chapter. Check out "Deflating Inflammation" (page 68) and Appendix B (page 186), and consider adding the recommended herbs to any morning recipe. No-Cook Morning Oatmeal (page 67) is fast and convenient, while the pancakes, scones, quiche, bars, and bites can all be prepared in advance, so that you can always leave home feeling satisfied.

< 51 >

Deflating Inflammation

>>>> Banana-Nut Mojo

Makes: 1 drink

1 cup coconut milk

2 bananas, cut into 2-inch chunks (fresh or frozen)

1 cup spinach leaves

2 tablespoons almond butter

2 teaspoons ground flaxseeds

1 teaspoon Canna Oil (page 15) or Canna Nut Butter (page 29)

½ teaspoon maca powder, optional (see Glossary, page 205)

¼ teaspoon ground cinnamon

— Combine the milk, bananas, spinach, almond butter, flaxseeds, Canna Oil, maca (if using), and cinnamon in a blender. Blend on high speed for 30 seconds, or until the ingredients are liquefied.

1 serving = 1 drink

DOSE: 1 Banana-Nut Mojo provides 4 to 6 mg THC if you have used the Recommended Carrier Amounts table (page 9) to make the Canna Oil.

>>>> Enrich Smoothie

Makes: 2 smoothies

1 cup almond milk

½ cup whole milk yogurt

¼ cup whole milk powder

2 teaspoons Canna Nut Butter (page 29)

½ banana, cut into chunks

½ cup frozen berries

¼ cup chopped dried dates or apricots

---

1 serving = 1 smoothie

DOSE: 1 Enrich Smoothie provides 4 to 6 mg THC if you have used the Recommended Carrier Amounts table (page 9) to make the Canna Nut Butter.

— Combine the almond milk, yogurt, milk powder, Canna Nut Butter, banana, berries, and dates in a blender. Process the mixture on high speed for 1 minute or until it is smooth.

Recipe Notes

- There is enough protein in this drink to hold you over until lunch. For a vegan version, substitute ½ cup soft tofu for the yogurt and whole milk powder.

- This recipe makes 1 very large drink. If you decide to drink all of it in one sitting, remember to use only 1 teaspoon Canna Nut Butter. You can add up to ¼ cup regular nut butter, but always be aware of the amount of Cannabis you are taking in a smoothie (or any other food).

- You can opt to make the recipe as it is, drink half, and refrigerate the rest to use the next day. You can also cut the ingredients in half to make a smaller drink for 1 serving.

- If you decide to store the remaining smoothie, keep it in a closed container (a jar or bottle with a lid) in the refrigerator and out of the reach of children. It's best to keep the smoothie for 1 day only—and remember to give it a shake before drinking.

>>>> Orange Creamsicle Smoothie

Makes: 1 smoothie

½ cup freshly squeezed orange juice

1 cup frozen vanilla yogurt

⅓ cup frozen orange juice concentrate

1 orange, peeled, seeded, and roughly chopped

1 packet (0.3 ounce) effervescent vitamin C powder, optional (see Recipe Note)

1 tablespoon CBD-rich hemp oil or 1 teaspoon Canna Honey (page 24)

---

1 serving = 1 smoothie

DOSE: 1 Orange Creamsicle Smoothie provides no THC if you use hemp oil, and 4 to 6 mg THC if you have used the Recommended Carrier Amounts table (page 9) to make the Canna Honey.

— Combine the juice, yogurt, juice concentrate, orange, vitamin C powder (if using), and hemp oil in a blender. Blend on high speed for 1 minute or until smooth.

Recipe Note

- You can find vitamin C powder in convenient, single-serve packets at the pharmacy or most grocery stores. I use them in smoothies or add them to water to boost vitamin C intake during cold and flu season. If you don't have any vitamin C powder on hand, you can simply omit it.

>>> Raw Cannabis Morning Juice

(a raw Cannabis recipe)

Makes: 1 drink, no THC

3 fresh Cannabis leaves

2 kale leaves

2 carrots

1 mango, peeled and pitted

1 orange, peeled

¼ cup plain yogurt, optional

— Using a juicer, process the Cannabis, kale, carrots, mango, and orange into the jug or container. Whisk in yogurt, if you're using it.

>>>> Wake-Up Smoothie

½ cup chilled pomegranate or cranberry juice

1 cup coarsely chopped dark leafy greens (see Recipe Note)

½ avocado, pitted and peeled

¼ cup blueberries, fresh or frozen

1 tablespoon Power Herb Cocoa Blend (page 174)

1 teaspoon Canna Oil (page 15) or Canna Coco Oil (page 13)

1 serving = 1 smoothie

DOSE: 1 Wake-Up Smoothie provides 5 mg THC if you have used the Recommended Carrier Amounts table (page 9) to make the Canna Oil.

— Combine the juice, greens, avocado, blueberries, Power Herb Cocoa Blend, and Canna Oil in a blender. Process for 1 minute or until the mixture is smooth and well combined.

Recipe Note

• Use fresh or frozen spinach, kale, Swiss chard, arugula, broccoli, or even cabbage leaves to add vitamins and minerals to this smoothie.

>>>> Canna Pancakes

Makes: 4 pancakes

⅓ cup large-flake rolled oats

2 tablespoons ground flaxseed

½ teaspoon baking powder

1 ripe banana, cut into chunks

1 tablespoon Canna Oil (page 15)

2 eggs

1 tablespoon extra-virgin avocado oil

1 cup mixed berries, fresh or thawed, if frozen (see Recipe Note below)

1 cup vanilla or plain yogurt, optional

Cheese Variation

⅔ cup shredded Cheddar cheese

1. Preheat the oven to 300°F (150°C).

2. Combine the oats, flaxseed, and baking powder in a food processor and process for 30 seconds. Add the banana, Canna Oil, and eggs, and process for 20 seconds or until the ingredients are well blended. Scrape the batter into a medium bowl using a rubber spatula. **Variation:** Add cheese to the batter and mix well.

3. Lightly oil a griddle or skillet with avocado oil and place the pan over medium-high heat. Drop the batter onto the hot pan using a 4-ounce (½ cup) ladle to form 2 or 3 pancakes. Cook for 1 or 2 minutes or until the pancakes are lightly browned around the edges and bubbles appear on top. Flip and cook the pancakes for 1 minute or until they have browned on the other side. Transfer the pancakes to a baking sheet, cover them with foil, and keep in the preheated oven to stay warm. Repeat the process until the remaining batter has been used up.

4. Serve the pancakes with fresh berries and yogurt (if using) on top.

---

1 serving = 2 pancakes

DOSE: **2 Canna Pancakes provide about 5 mg THC if you have used the Recommended Carrier Amounts table (page 9) to make the Canna Oil.**

STORAGE: **Stack cooled pancakes between parchment paper and freeze in a labeled, resealable bag for up to 3 months.**

TO REHEAT: **Pop a pancake into the toaster (no need to thaw).**

Recipe Note

- Fresh berries (blueberries, raspberries, blackberries, cherries, strawberries) are best, but you can use frozen berries if that's all you have (be sure to thaw and drain them first).

>>>> Cheesy Scones

2 cups all-purpose flour

1 tablespoon baking powder

½ teaspoon sea salt

¼ cup chilled Canna Coco Oil (page 13), cut into small pieces (see Recipe Note opposite)

1 cup grated Cheddar cheese

1 cup chilled milk

---

1 serving = 1 scone

DOSE: 1 Cheesy Scone provides about 5 mg THC if you have used the Recommended Carrier Amounts table (page 9) to make the Canna Coco Oil.

STORAGE: Stack cooled scones between parchment paper and place them in an airtight container. Scones will keep in the refrigerator for up to 1 week or in the freezer, in a labeled resealable bag, for up to 3 months.

---

1. Preheat the oven to 450°F (230°C). Lightly grease a rimmed baking sheet.

2. Combine the flour, baking powder, and salt in a large bowl and stir with a fork. Cut the chilled pieces of the Canna Coco Oil into the flour mixture using a pastry cutter or kitchen knives. Work in the oil until the pieces are about the size of peas. Stir in the cheese and toss to mix well.

3. Make a well in the center of the mixture and pour in the milk. Stir just until all the flour mixture has been moistened. Turn out onto a floured cutting board. Roll the dough into a rectangle about ¾ inch thick.

4. Using a 2-inch round cookie cutter, cut 12 circles and transfer them to the prepared baking sheet, allowing an inch of space around each circle. Bake the scones in the preheated oven for 10 to 12 minutes or until they've turned golden.

- The nature of the dough requires that you cut chilled fat into the dry ingredients so that as the scones bake, the fat melts and keeps the scones moist and airy. Liquid oil or ghee won't work as well as Canna Coco Oil that has been chilled for about half an hour.

Ginger Bites

⅓ cup pure maple syrup

¼ cup blackstrap molasses

⅓ cup Canna Oil (page 15)

3 tablespoons finely chopped peeled fresh ginger

½ teaspoon ground cinnamon

¼ teaspoon ground allspice

¼ teaspoon ground coriander

1⅓ cups spelt flour or all-purpose flour

½ teaspoon baking powder

½ teaspoon baking soda

¼ teaspoon sea salt

Granulated sugar, for rolling

---

1 serving = 1 bite

DOSE: 1 Ginger Bite provides about 4 mg THC if you have used the Recommended Carrier Amounts table (page 9) to make the Canna Oil.

STORAGE: Ginger Bites will keep in an airtight container in the refrigerator for up to 14 days.

TO FREEZE: Arrange Ginger Bites in a single layer on a baking sheet and freeze for 30 minutes. Transfer the bites to a resealable bag or freezer container. Seal, label, and freeze the container. Frozen bites will keep for up to 3 months.

---

1. Preheat the oven to 350°F (180°C). Line 2 baking sheets with parchment paper.

2. Combine the maple syrup, molasses, Canna Oil, ginger, cinnamon, allspice, and coriander in a saucepan. Place the pan over medium heat, stirring the mixture constantly, for 1 minute. Remove the pan from the heat and set it aside to cool until lukewarm.

3. Combine the flour, baking powder, baking soda, and salt in a large bowl. Scrape the maple syrup mixture into the flour mixture using a rubber spatula and stir until the mixture forms a firm dough.

4. Place about ¼ cup of sugar in a shallow dish and set it aside. Measure 2 tablespoons of dough using a lightly oiled tablespoon (or a 1-ounce ice-cream scoop) and roll it between your palms to make a ball. Drop the ball into the sugar. Roll the ball in the sugar until it is completely covered. Transfer the ball to the prepared baking sheet. Repeat, spacing each ball 2 inches apart. Using the oiled tines of a fork, flatten each bite slightly.

5. Bake the ginger bites in the preheated oven for 10 to 12 minutes or until they are crisp and lightly browned. Let them cool on the pan for 5 minutes before transferring them to a wire rack to cool completely

6. Transfer the bites to an airtight container. Seal, label, and keep the container in the refrigerator, out of the reach of children.

>>> Mini-Quiche with Arugula and Smoked Salmon

Makes: 12 mini-quiches

¼ cup Canna Ghee (page 16), Canna Oil (page 15), or Canna Coco Oil (page 13)

1½ cups finely diced sweet potato or regular potato

1 onion, finely diced

½ teaspoon sea salt, divided

8 large eggs

½ cup half-and-half or full-fat milk

1 cup roughly chopped arugula or spinach

1 cup diced smoked salmon

1. Preheat the oven to 325°F (160°C). Lightly oil a 12-cup muffin pan.

2. Heat the Canna Ghee in a skillet over medium-high heat. Add the potato and onion, and cook, stirring frequently, for 5 minutes. Remove the pan from the heat and stir in ¼ teaspoon salt. Set the pan aside to cool.

3. Whisk together the eggs, half-and-half, and remaining salt in a large bowl. Stir in the arugula or spinach, the salmon, and the cooled potato mixture. Divide the quiche mixture evenly among the prepared muffin cups.

4. Bake the mini-quiches for 25 minutes or until they are firm to the touch. Let the quiches rest in the pan for 5 minutes, and then serve or transfer them to a wire rack to cool.

1 serving = 1 mini-quiche

DOSE: 1 Mini-Quiche provides about 5 mg THC if you have used the Recommended Carrier Amounts table (page 9) to make the Canna Ghee.

STORAGE: Mini-Quiches will keep in an airtight container in the refrigerator for up to 1 week.

TO FREEZE: Wrap each quiche in foil. Label and freeze them in a resealable bag for up to 3 months.

TO REHEAT: Thaw 1 or more quiche in the refrigerator overnight. Heat the quiche, wrapped in foil, at 325°F (160°C) for 10 minutes or until warmed through.

➤➤➤ Individual Coffee Cakes

Coffee Cakes

1 cup all-purpose flour

¼ cup granulated sugar

1 teaspoon baking powder

½ teaspoon salt

¼ cup Canna Ghee (page 16) or Canna Oil (page 15)

1 egg

¼ cup regular milk or almond milk

1 teaspoon pure vanilla extract

Topping

⅓ cup packed brown sugar

2 tablespoons large-flake rolled oats

½ teaspoon ground cinnamon

2 tablespoons melted butter

1. Preheat the oven to 350°F (180°C) and lightly oil a 12-cup muffin pan.

2. *To make the coffee cakes:* Combine the flour, sugar, baking powder, and salt in a large bowl. Make a well in the dry mixture and add the Canna Ghee, mixing it in with a fork. Add the egg, milk, and vanilla and mix just until all the dry ingredients are incorporated.

3. Using a ½-cup measure, scoop the batter into the prepared muffin pan.

4. *To make the topping:* Combine the sugar, oatmeal, cinnamon, and butter in a medium bowl. Mix with a fork until the topping is crumbly. Spoon about 2 teaspoons over each mini-cake.

5. Bake them in the preheated oven for 15 to 20 minutes or until a cake tester comes out clean when inserted into the center of a mini-cake.

1 serving = 1 mini-cake

DOSE: 1 Individual Coffee Cake provides about 5 mg THC if you have used the Recommended Carrier Amounts table (page 9) to make the Canna Oil.

STORAGE: Freeze Individual Coffee Cakes in a labeled resealable bag for up to 3 months.

No-Bake Energy Bars

2 cups large-flake rolled oats

½ cup flaked or shredded unsweetened coconut

½ cup chopped almonds

¼ cup Canna Ghee (page 16) or Canna Coco Oil (page 13)

¼ cup liquid honey

1 teaspoon pure vanilla extract

¼ cup chopped pitted dates

1 cup chopped dried apricots or apples

2 tablespoons ground flaxseeds

1 tablespoon ground cinnamon

½ teaspoon ground allspice

---

1 serving = 2 bars

DOSE: 2 No-Bake Energy Bars provide about 5 mg THC if you have used the Recommended Carrier Amounts table (page 9) to make the Canna Ghee.

STORAGE: No-Bake Energy Bars will keep for up to 3 weeks in an airtight container in the refrigerator or up to 3 months in the freezer.

TO FREEZE: Transfer the wrapped bars to an airtight container or a resealable freezer bag. Seal, label, and freeze the bars for up to 3 months.

1. Preheat the oven to 350°F (180°C). Line a rimmed baking sheet and a large baking pan with parchment paper (see Recipe Notes below).

2. Spread the oats, coconut, and almonds on the prepared baking sheet. Toast the mixture in the preheated oven for 5 minutes. Stir, and return the mixture to the oven for 3 to 5 minutes or until it is lightly browned. Set it aside to cool.

3. Combine the Canna Ghee, honey, and vanilla in a large saucepan over medium-high heat. When small bubbles form around the inside of the pan, add the dates. Cook the mixture, stirring constantly, for 6 minutes or until the dates are soft and have been thoroughly incorporated into the honey mixture.

4. Add the apricots, flaxseeds, cinnamon, and allspice to the cooled oat mixture on the baking sheet and stir them in. Drizzle the hot honey mixture on top and stir it into the mixture on the baking sheet until it is completely incorporated. Press the mixture evenly into the prepared baking pan, cover it with plastic wrap, and refrigerate for at least 2 hours or until the mixture is firm.

5. Cut the mixture into 24 bars and wrap each bar individually in parchment paper or plastic wrap (see Recipe Notes below). Store the bars in an airtight container in the refrigerator, out of the reach of children.

Recipe Notes

- Use a 9 x 12-inch or 13-inch baking pan to make the energy bars. If you use a smaller pan, the length and width of the bars will be smaller but the height will be larger. Either way, be sure to cut 24 even bars (use a ruler) so that the dose is consistent per bar.

- This is a good recipe to try microdosing (see page 11) because 1 bar provides about 2.5 mg THC.

No-Cook Morning Oatmeal

2 cups almond milk

2 teaspoons Canna Nut Butter (page 29)

1 cup large-flake rolled oats

½ cup dried blueberries or cranberries

3 tablespoons unsweetened dark cocoa powder, optional

2 tablespoons chia seeds

½ teaspoon ground cinnamon

½ banana, sliced, and/or pure maple syrup or honey, optional, to serve

---

1 serving = 1 cup

DOSE: 1 cup No-Cook Morning Oatmeal provides about 5 mg THC if you have used the Recommended Carrier Amounts table (page 9) to make the Canna Nut Butter.

STORAGE: No-Cook Morning Oatmeal will keep for up to 2 days in an airtight container in the refrigerator.

---

1. In a jar, combine the milk and Canna Nut Butter. Shake the jar vigorously to thoroughly mix the ingredients. Add oats, blueberries, cocoa powder (if using), chia seeds, and cinnamon. Shake to mix well.

2. Refrigerate the jar overnight. Serve the oatmeal chilled or at room temperature, topped with sliced bananas and drizzled with maple syrup or honey, if desired.

DEFLATING INFLAMMATION

Inflammation is the body's primary defense mechanism against infection and wounds, and it always starts out as a way of protecting and eliminating the initial cause of cell injury. We all agree: This is a good and natural thing.

However, inflammation becomes a problem when it gets to be chronic, when it continues after the initial crisis has passed. Chronic inflammation is a major factor in the development of degenerative conditions such as heart disease, cancer, Alzheimer's, diabetes, migraines, thyroid, and dental issues.

Anti-Inflammatory Foods

Dark-colored fruits and vegetables are high in anti-inflammatory, antioxidant anthocyanins that help prevent oxidative stress from extreme physical exertion. Eat blueberries; kale and other dark leafy greens; red and green peppers; broccoli, purple cabbage, and other cruciferous vegetables; tomatoes; red, black, and blue berries; black plums; and black cherries.

Pineapple makes a good treat because it contains bromelain, an enzyme that aids in digestion and is anti-inflammatory.

Eat omega-3 fatty acid–rich foods, such as almonds, walnuts, flaxseeds, and fatty fish (wild salmon, mackerel, sardines), because they help reduce inflammation.

Matcha is a powder made from a high grade of unfermented green tea leaves. It's rich in antioxidants but contains caffeine. To make traditional matcha, combine 1 teaspoon matcha powder with ⅓ cup boiled water in a small teacup. Whisk to a froth using a small whisk or bamboo brush.

Shiitake mushrooms contain the amino acid ergothioneine, which inhibits oxidative stress and may reduce inflammation.

To get started in the mornings, try these recipes, which are anti-inflammatory due to the cannabinoids and herbs. Also enjoy other anti-inflammatory drinks, such as Green CBD Smoothie (page 81), Golden Latte (page 169), and Iced Golden Smoothie (page 170). For a list of anti-inflammatory herbs, see page 195.

Anti-Inflammatory Matcha Tea Blend

(a loose tea blend)

Makes: 1 cup, no THC

½ cup chopped dried blueberries

2 tablespoons matcha green tea powder

3 tablespoons chopped fresh or ground turmeric

1 tablespoon ground cinnamon

1 tablespoon ground ginger

— Combine the blueberries, matcha, turmeric, cinnamon, and ginger in a jar and shake to mix. Seal, label, and store the tea in a cool, dark cupboard.

STEEPED ANTI-INFLAMMATORY MATCHA TEA

(per cup of tea)

Makes: 1 cup

1 tablespoon Anti-Inflammatory Matcha Tea Blend (see recipe above), or to taste

1 cup hot water

1 teaspoon Canna Honey (page 24) or Canna Oil (page 15)

1. Measure the tea blend into a small teapot or heatproof jar with a lid. Pour the hot water on top. Cover the teapot or jar and let the tea steep for 5 minutes.

2. Strain the steeped tea through a fine-mesh strainer into a cup or a small glass and stir in the Canna Honey. Drink the tea immediately or cover and refrigerate (out of the reach of children).

Recipe Notes

- THC isn't water-soluble, so always add a 1-teaspoon dose of Canna Honey (page 24), Canna Oil (page 15), or Canna Tincture (page 33–34) to impart the medicinal or psychoactive compounds to the tea.

- Add 1 tablespoon (or to taste) of the Anti-Inflammatory Matcha Tea Blend to a serving of juice or a smoothie.

1 serving = 1 cup

DOSE: 1 cup of Steeped Anti-Inflammatory Matcha Tea provides 5 mg THC if you have used the Recommended Carrier Amounts table (page 9) to make Canna Honey.

->>>> Golden Elixir

2 teaspoons Canna Honey
(page 24) or Canna Oil
(page 15)

2 teaspoons ground turmeric

½ teaspoon ground ginger

Pinch of ground cloves

2 cups vanilla-flavored
almond milk

Pinch of freshly ground
black pepper

½ teaspoon ground
cinnamon, for garnish,
optional

---

1 serving = 1 drink

DOSE: 1 Golden Elixir
provides about 5 mg
THC if you have used the
Recommended Carrier
Amounts table (page 9) to
make the Canna Honey.

---

1. Heat the Canna Honey in a saucepan over medium heat. Add the turmeric, ginger, and cloves, and stir until a smooth paste forms. Gradually add the almond milk and pepper to the Canna Honey mixture, whisking constantly, until small bubbles form around the inside of the pan.

2. Set aside to cool slightly, then divide the mixture evenly between two glasses and garnish with a sprinkle of cinnamon (if using).

Recipe Note

- If you are taking Cannabis to help alleviate inflammation, consider making Ayurvedic Canna Butter (page 27) and use it in place of Canna Honey or Canna Oil in this recipe.

Breakfast Smoothie

Makes: 2 smoothies

1 cup unsweetened almond milk

¼ cup skim milk powder

1 banana, cut into chunks

1 cup frozen mixed berries (blueberries, blackberries, cherries, strawberries)

½ cup chopped dark leafy greens

2 teaspoons Canna Nut Butter (page 29) or Canna Coco Oil (page 13); (see Recipe Notes)

1 tablespoon dark chocolate cocoa powder

1 teaspoon ground turmeric

---

1 serving = 1 smoothie

DOSE: 1 Breakfast Smoothie provides 4 to 6 mg THC if you have used the Recommended Carrier Amounts table (page 9) to make the Canna Nut Butter.

— Combine the milk, milk powder, banana, berries, greens, Canna Nut Butter, cocoa, and turmeric in a blender. Process on high speed for 30 seconds or until liquefied.

Recipe Notes

- Every ingredient in this smoothie is there because it helps get you going and ready to perform. For example, caffeine in chocolate dilates and relaxes blood vessels, which helps oxygen-rich blood reach your brain and muscles fast, and turmeric is an anti-inflammatory power herb.

- This recipe makes one very large drink. If you decide to enjoy the drink in one sitting, remember to use only 1 teaspoon Canna Nut Butter. You can add up to ¼ cup regular nut butter, but always be aware of the amount of Cannabis you are taking in a smoothie or anything else you eat or drink.

- You can opt to make the recipe as is, drink half, and refrigerate the rest to use the next day. You can also cut the ingredients in half to make a smaller drink for 1 serving.

- If you store the remaining smoothie, keep it in a closed container (a jar or a drink bottle with a lid) in the refrigerator, and out of the reach of children. It's best to drink it the same day—and remember to shake the smoothie before drinking it.

>>>> Joint Pain Relief Body Rub

(for external use only)

1 cup chopped mullein roots
(see Resources, page 210)
or turmeric, fresh or dried

½ ounce (14 grams)
activated CBD-rich
Cannabis

2 cups body oil blend
(almond oil, hemp oil,
avocado oil, or grapeseed
oil; or a blend of one or
more)

1 teaspoon fragrant
essential oil (rose or
lavender), optional

1. Combine the mullein, Cannabis, and body oil in a 1-quart Mason jar. Seal the jar and set it aside. Line a small slow cooker with a dish towel, folded lengthwise into fourths. Place the jar on the towel. Pour warm water into the slow cooker until it reaches about an inch above the oil in the jar.

2. Set the temperature on low and cover with the lid. Heat the oil for 4 days. On day 5, unplug the slow cooker. Let the jar cool to the touch before transferring it to a wire rack to cool completely.

3. Line a fine-mesh strainer with a double layer of cheesecloth or a basket-style paper coffee filter. Set the strainer over a 2-cup liquid measuring cup and pour the oil through the strainer into the measuring cup. Be patient and let the oil drip through, without squeezing or pressing on the filter, and discard the solids. Add the essential oil (if using) to the infused oil and stir well.

4. Pour the oil into a 2-cup Mason jar or several smaller dropper bottles. Seal, label, and store in a cool, dark cupboard, out of the reach of children.

Recipe Notes

- This oil should be high in CBD and low in THC, and is used topically, so there is no restriction on the amount you use.

- For relief from pain, rub a tablespoon of the oil into your fingers, wrist, knees, shoulders, or other joints, or have someone massage the oil into your spine or lower back.

>>>> Joint Relief Bites

⅔ cup large-flake rolled oats

1 medium carrot, grated

½ cup coarsely chopped pitted dates

½ cup chopped dried cherries or cranberries

½ cup walnut pieces

¼ cup Canna Nut Butter (page 29)

½ teaspoon ground ginger

¼ teaspoon ground turmeric

Pinch of sea salt

1 tablespoon pomegranate juice or orange juice

---

1 serving = 2 bites

DOSE: 2 Joint Relief Bites provide about 6 mg THC if you have used the Recommended Carrier Amounts table (page 9) to make the Canna Nut Butter.

STORAGE: Joint Relief Bites will keep in an airtight container in the refrigerator for up to 1 week.

TO FREEZE: Arrange the bites in a single layer on a rimmed baking sheet and freeze them for 30 minutes. Transfer the bites to a resealable bag. Label the bag and keep it in the freezer for up to 4 months.

1. Line a rimmed baking sheet with parchment paper. Set it aside.

2. Combine the oats, carrots, dates, cherries, and walnuts in a food processor. Process for 30 seconds or until the dried berries and walnuts are chopped and the ingredients are evenly distributed. Add the Canna Nut Butter, ginger, turmeric, salt, and juice. Process until the mixture comes together in a smooth ball.

3. Using a 1-tablespoon measure, scoop up some of the mixture, press it against the side of the bowl to pack it firmly, and then scrape the packed mixture out of the tablespoon and onto the prepared baking sheet. Repeat until the mixture has been used up.

4. Transfer the bites to an airtight container. Label the container and keep it in the refrigerator, out of the reach of children.

CHAPTER 3

< **SNACKS** >

It seems that, being human, we all fall victim to the same mistake: We eat too much Cannabis-infused food at one time. The good news is, it only happens once. But you can keep it from ever happening if you are patient and conscious of the amount of THC you put into every bite. It's helpful to remember that it takes longer for THC in edibles to be felt, and the effects may come on stronger and last longer than if you were to vape or smoke the same amount of THC.

Remember, too, that if you are hungry and grab a Cannabis-infused snack, the effect will be different than if you had just eaten a meal and consumed the same snack. An empty stomach definitely allows you to feel the effects of THC much more quickly, and perhaps with more intensity. So, with snacks, it's worth repeating: Start low and go slow.

You may also find that when smoothies or other drinks are made with Canna Honey (page 24) and taken as snacks, the THC may be absorbed in the mouth and therefore will reach the bloodstream relatively quickly. On the other hand, when THC is contained in fat-infused ingredients—coconut oil, olive oil, butter, cream, or nut butter—and those ingredients are eaten alone or in food, the THC is processed by the liver, which increases the length of time it takes to feel any effect. Interestingly, the liver converts THC to 11-hydroxy THC, which easily crosses the blood-brain barrier and produces a more intense high.

All this is to say that you can't mindlessly pop or sip Cannabis-infused snacks. Instead, take the following snacks along with a dose of common sense.

< 77 >

Cannabis at the Spa

Cool-Down Smoothie

¾ cup unsweetened almond milk

½ cup tart cherry juice

1 cup roughly chopped papaya, fresh or frozen

1 cup roughly chopped black plums

1 cup frozen berries (blueberries, blackberries, strawberries)

1 banana, broken into 3 pieces

1 piece (½ to ¾ inch) fresh turmeric, roughly chopped, or ½ teaspoon ground turmeric

1 piece (1 inch) fresh ginger, roughly chopped

2 teaspoons Canna Coco Oil (page 13) or Canna Healing Honey (page 25); (see Recipe Notes)

Juice of ½ lemon

Pinch of ground cinnamon

1 serving = 1 smoothie

DOSE: 1 Cool-Down Smoothie provides 4 to 6 mg THC if you have used the Recommended Carrier Amounts table (page 9) to make the Canna Coco Oil.

— Combine the milk, cherry juice, papaya, plums, berries, banana, turmeric, ginger, Canna Coco Oil, lemon juice, and cinnamon in a blender. Process on high speed for 30 seconds or until liquefied.

Recipe Notes

- Tart cherry juice and turmeric help prevent inflammation and reduce muscle soreness—perfect for after workouts.

- This recipe makes one very large drink or two smaller ones. If you decide to enjoy the whole drink in one sitting, use only 1 teaspoon of Canna Coco Oil. Always be aware of the amount of Cannabis you are ingesting in a drink or in food.

- You can opt to make the recipe as is, drink half, and refrigerate the rest to use later in the day. You can also cut the ingredients in half to make a smaller drink for 1 serving.

- If you store the remaining smoothie, keep it in a closed container (a jar or a bottle with a lid) in the refrigerator and out of the reach of children. It's best to drink it the same day—and remember to shake the smoothie before drinking it.

- If you decide to make only half the recipe, note that, for the almond milk, half of ¾ cup is 6 tablespoons.

Makes: 3 cups

¼ ounce (7 grams) chopped activated Cannabis (see Recipe Notes below)

½ cup chopped berries (fresh or frozen blueberries, blackberries, strawberries, cherries, raspberries)

¼ cup chopped fresh hawthorn berries, leaves, or flowers, optional

1 small orange, rind on, sliced

3 tablespoons chopped fresh or dried rose hips

2 tablespoons Siberian ginseng, optional

1 tablespoon grated fresh ginger

1 stick (2 inches) cinnamon

3 cups brandy or vodka (40%–45% alcohol)

¼ cup liquid honey or maple syrup, to taste, optional

1 serving = 1 teaspoon or 20 drops

DOSE: 1 teaspoon or 20 drops of Energy Tonic will provide about 5 mg THC if you use a strain of Cannabis that is between 10% and 12% THC and 3 cups of brandy.

1. Combine the Cannabis, berries, hawthorn (if using), orange slices, rose hips, ginseng (if using), ginger, and cinnamon in a wide-mouth quart jar. Pour the brandy on top, making sure it covers the ingredients. Seal, label, and store the jar at room temperature, away from direct sunlight and heat and out of the reach of children, for 1 month, shaking the jar once a day or every few days, whenever you remember.

2. Line a fine-mesh strainer with 2 layers of cheesecloth or a basket-style paper coffee filter and set it over a 1-quart measuring cup or bowl. Pour the tonic from the jar into the strainer, pressing on the fruit and herbs to extract as much liquid as possible. Gather the corners of the cheesecloth and twist and squeeze the fruit and herbs to release as much infused brandy as possible. Transfer the solids to a jar. Seal, label, and store the jar in the refrigerator—out of the reach of children—to use in smoothies (see Recipe Notes below).

3. Taste the tonic and stir in up to ¼ cup of honey if desired. Pour the tonic into a jar with a lid. Label and store the jar in a cool, dark cupboard out of the reach of children. Take a dose just after breakfast or in the afternoon.

Recipe Notes

- Use a sativa strain of Cannabis with 10%–12% THC, if possible.

- Keep the strained herbs out of the reach of children and blend 1 teaspoon into smoothies that have no other source of THC.

>>>> Green CBD Smoothie

½ cup light (5% butterfat) cream or almond milk

2 cups chopped leafy greens (kale, spinach, chard)

½ cup chopped broccoli florets

2 tablespoons unsalted almonds

2 tablespoons chopped fresh parsley

1 to 2 teaspoons high-CBD Canna Oil (page 15), Energy Tonic (opposite), or Canna Coco Oil (page 13); (see Recipe Note)

1 serving = 1 smoothie

DOSE: 1 Green CBD Smoothie provides 17 to 18 mg CBD and a much lower amount (about 5 mg) of THC, if you have used a high-CBD ratio of Cannabis and followed the Recommended Carrier Amounts table (page 9) to make the Canna Oil.

— Combine the cream, greens, broccoli, almonds, parsley, and Canna Oil in a blender. Process on high speed for 1 minute or until smooth.

Recipe Note

- If you are using a high-CBD (20%) strain with very low THC (0% to 6%), such as Low Tide from Green Relief, you could use 1 to 2 teaspoons of Canna Oil in this drink. Start with 1 teaspoon and gauge the effect. Write down the results and, if you wish, try increasing the amount by ½ teaspoon each time.

>>>> Almond Squares

Makes: 16 squares

5 tablespoons Canna Ghee (page 16) or Canna Coco Oil (page 13)

3 eggs

⅔ cup ground almonds

1½ cups whole milk powder

¾ cup granulated sugar

½ teaspoon ground turmeric

---

1 serving = 1 square

DOSE: 1 Almond Square provides about 4 mg THC if you have used the Recommended Carrier Amounts table (page 9) to make the Canna Ghee.

STORAGE: Almond squares will keep for up to 14 days in an airtight container in the refrigerator.

TO FREEZE: Place the squares on a rimmed baking sheet and freeze them for 30 minutes. Transfer the squares to a resealable bag. Label the bag and keep it in the freezer for up to 3 months.

1. Preheat the oven to 325°F (160°C). Lightly oil an 8-inch-square baking pan.

2. Melt the Canna Ghee in a saucepan over low heat. When the ghee has melted, turn the heat off and leave the pan on the burner.

3. Beat the eggs together in a bowl and set them aside.

4. Combine the almonds, milk powder, sugar, and turmeric in a food processor and pour the melted Canna Ghee on top. Pulse the ingredients 2 or 3 times, until they're well combined. Add the eggs and pulse 2 or 3 times to mix well.

5. Use a rubber spatula to scrape the mixture into the prepared pan and smooth the top. Bake the mixture in the preheated oven for 45 minutes or until a toothpick inserted into the center comes out clean.

6. Transfer the pan to a wire rack to cool for 30 minutes. Lift out the baked almond mixture and cut it into sixteen 2-inch squares (use a ruler). Place the squares in an airtight container. Seal, label, and keep the container in the refrigerator, out of the reach of children.

>>> Canna Nut Goof Balls

¼ cup Canna Coco Oil (page 13) or Canna Oil (page 15)

2 squares (0.35 ounces each) chocolate, 85% cacao

½ cup nut butter

¼ cup coconut nectar

3 cups crumbled rice cakes (see Recipe Notes below)

½ cup finely chopped pitted dates

½ cup large-flake rolled oats

3 tablespoons unsalted sunflower seeds or chopped walnuts

2 tablespoons unsweetened cocoa powder

1 teaspoon ground power herb, optional (see Recipe Notes)

½ teaspoon ground cinnamon

1. Line a rimmed baking sheet with parchment paper.

2. Place the Canna Coco Oil and chocolate squares in a saucepan over medium-low heat, stirring frequently, until the oil and chocolate have melted. Remove the pan from the heat and stir in the nut butter and coconut nectar. Set the pan aside to cool.

3. Meanwhile, combine the rice cake crumbs, dates, oats, sunflower seeds, cocoa, power herb (if using), and cinnamon in a food processor and pulse 2 or 3 times. Scrape the Canna Coco Oil mixture into the food processor bowl, along with the dry ingredients. Process for 10 seconds or until all the ingredients are well combined.

4. Measure 2 tablespoons and drop the mixture onto the prepared baking sheet. Repeat to make 12 balls. Refrigerate the balls on the baking sheet for an hour or until they're firm. Transfer the balls to an airtight container and refrigerate or freeze them.

---

1 serving = 1 ball

DOSE: 1 Canna Nut Goof Ball provides about 5 mg THC if you have used the Recommended Carrier Amounts table (page 9) to make the Canna Coco Oil.

STORAGE: Canna Nut Goof Balls will keep in an airtight container in the refrigerator for up to 1 week.

TO FREEZE: Arrange the balls in a single layer on a parchment-lined rimmed baking sheet and freeze for 30 minutes. Transfer to a resealable bag or container, seal and label the bag, and keep it in the freezer for up to 3 months.

Recipe Notes

- For this recipe, I prefer to use salted brown rice cakes, but experiment with the type you like. If you use unsalted rice cakes, you may wish to add ½ teaspoon sea salt in step 2. To crumble rice cakes: Place the cakes between 2 pieces of parchment paper and use a rolling pin to crush them.

- See herbs for symptom relief in Appendix B (page 186) and add one herb to this recipe if desired.

>>> Avocado Tostadas

Makes: 2 tostadas

2 cloves garlic

1 fresh jalapeño pepper, roughly chopped

4 scallions, roughly chopped

1 handful fresh cilantro or parsley leaves

1 tablespoon Canna Oil (page 15) or Canna Coco Oil (page 13)

2 ripe avocados

½ fresh lime or lemon, freshly squeezed

2 large (10-inch) tortillas

1 tablespoon extra-virgin olive oil

1 cup shredded green or red cabbage

1 tomato, cut into 8 pieces

¼ cup shredded Cheddar cheese

¼ cup toasted walnuts

---

1 serving = 1 tostada

DOSE: 1 Avocado Tostada provides about 6 mg THC if you have used the Recommended Carrier Amounts table (page 9) to make the Canna Oil.

1. Turn on the oven broiler. Line a baking sheet with parchment paper.

2. Combine the garlic, pepper, scallions, cilantro, and Canna Oil in a food processor or blender. Process on high for 10 seconds.

3. Cut the avocados in half and remove and discard the pits. Scoop the flesh out and add it to mixture in the blender. Drizzle lime juice over the mixture and process for 20 to 30 seconds or until it has the consistency of a rough paste with some visible chunks.

4. Brush the tortillas with oil on both sides and place them on the prepared baking sheet. Position the sheet under the broiler and toast the tortillas for 1 minute on each side or until crisp and golden at the edges. Place each tortilla on a serving plate.

5. Divide the avocado mixture in half and spread each tortilla with half of the mixture, leaving a 1-inch border around the edges. Spread ½ cup cabbage and 4 tomato pieces on each tortilla. Sprinkle half of the cheese and half of the walnuts over each of the tortillas.

Carrot Latkes

Makes: 8 latkes

3 tablespoons Canna Coco Oil (page 13) or Canna Oil (page 15)

1 large egg, lightly beaten

2 medium carrots, shredded (about ¾ cup)

1 stalk celery, shredded (about ⅓ cup)

½ onion, shredded (about ½ cup)

3 tablespoons chickpea flour or plain breadcrumbs

¼ cup chopped fresh parsley

½ teaspoon sea salt

1 to 2 tablespoons extra-virgin olive oil

---

1 serving = 1 latke

DOSE: **1 Carrot Latke provides about 5 mg THC if you have used the Recommended Carrier Amounts table (page 9) to make the Canna Coco Oil.**

STORAGE: **Carrot Latkes will keep in an airtight container in the refrigerator for up to 1 week and in the freezer for up to 5 months.**

---

1. Line a rimmed baking sheet with parchment paper.

2. Place the Canna Coco Oil and egg in a medium bowl. Using a fork, whisk the oil and egg. Add the carrots, celery, onion, flour, parsley, and salt. Scoop a heaping tablespoon of the mixture and press it between your palms to form a 2-inch patty. Repeat, placing the patties on the prepared baking sheet.

3. Heat 1 tablespoon of the olive oil in a large skillet over medium-high heat. Add 4 patties to the skillet and cook them until they turn golden brown, about 3 minutes per side. Transfer the patties to a serving platter and cook the remaining patties, adding more oil to the skillet, if needed.

>>>> Canna Roasted Red Pepper Hummus

Makes: about 3 cups

1 can (16 ounces) chickpeas

2 tablespoons Canna Oil (page 15) or Canna Coco Oil (page 13)

¼ cup unsalted hulled sunflower seeds

3 cloves garlic

2 tablespoons tahini (sesame paste)

2 tablespoons freshly squeezed lemon juice

1 roasted bell pepper

½ teaspoon sea salt

---

1 serving = ½ cup

DOSE: ½ cup Canna Roasted Red Pepper Hummus provides about 5 mg THC if you have used the Recommended Carrier Amounts table (page 9) to make the Canna Oil.

STORAGE: Hummus will keep in the refrigerator in an airtight container for up to 1 week.

TO FREEZE: Divide the remaining hummus into ½-cup portions and spoon them into resealable bags or freezer containers. Seal, label, and freeze for up to 5 months. Thaw in the refrigerator overnight before using.

---

1. Set a colander over a bowl and drain the chickpeas. Reserve the liquid. Rinse the chickpeas under cool running water and set them aside.

2. Combine the Canna Oil, sunflower seeds, and garlic in the bowl of a food processor. Pulse for 20 seconds or until the seeds are chopped. Add the tahini, lemon juice, bell pepper, salt, and drained chickpeas and process for 30 seconds. Using a rubber spatula, scrape down the sides of the bowl. With the motor running, add the reserved chickpea liquid, 1 tablespoon at a time, through the feed tube. Process the mixture until it is smooth (the more liquid you add, the thinner the mixture will be).

Chile Tapenade

Makes: 1¾ cups

2 cloves garlic

1 cayenne or jalapeño pepper, fresh or dried

1 cup pitted black or green olives

½ cup coarsely chopped fresh parsley

⅓ cup pine nuts

2 tablespoons Canna Oil (page 15)

1 teaspoon ground cumin

Juice of ½ lime

1 serving = ¼ cup

DOSE: ¼ cup Chile Tapenade provides about 4 mg THC if you have used the Recommended Carrier Amounts table (page 9) to make the Canna Oil.

STORAGE: Transfer the tapenade to an airtight container. Label the container and keep it in the refrigerator, out of the reach of children, for up to 8 days.

1. Combine the garlic and pepper in a food processor and pulse for 30 seconds or until the ingredients are chopped.

2. Add the olives, parsley, nuts, Canna Oil, and cumin. Process for 30 to 40 seconds or until the mixture is well blended.

3. Transfer the mixture to a bowl and stir in the lime juice.

Recipe Note

- Toss ¼ cup Chile Tapenade with 1 serving cooked pasta or serve with crackers or bread; use as a condiment for roasted vegetables or Baked Chicken Wings (page 107); or add to the stuffing in place of the Canna Oil in the Tomatoes Stuffed with Tuna recipe (page 137).

Flax and Walnut Oat Cookies

Makes: 14 cookies

½ cup all-purpose flour or gluten-free flour blend

½ cup large-flake rolled oats

½ cup coconut sugar or brown sugar

⅓ cup chopped walnuts

¼ cup ground flaxseed

¼ cup Canna Ghee (page 16) or Canna Coco Oil (page 13)

2 tablespoons unsalted butter, at room temperature

1 egg

1 serving = 1 cookie

DOSE: 1 Flax and Walnut Oat Cookie provides about 4 mg THC if you have used the Recommended Carrier Amounts table (page 9) to make the Canna Ghee.

STORAGE: Transfer cooled cookies to an airtight container. Label and refrigerate the container, out of the reach of children, for up to 1 week.

TO FREEZE: Arrange cookies in a single layer on a baking sheet and freeze for 30 minutes. Transfer the cookies to a resealable bag. Seal and label the bag, and keep it in the freezer for up to 4 months.

1. Preheat the oven to 350°F (180°C). Line two baking sheets with parchment paper.

2. Combine the flour, oats, sugar, walnuts, and flaxseed in a food processor. Process for 30 seconds or until oats and nuts are finely chopped.

3. Add the Canna Ghee, butter, and egg. Process for 30 seconds or until the mixture forms a soft dough.

4. Scoop 2 tablespoons of the dough, roll it into a ball, and place it on one of the prepared baking sheets. Continue to roll and place balls on the baking sheets, spacing them 2 inches apart, in 1 layer, until the dough is used up. Lightly flatten the balls using a fork.

5. Bake 1 sheet at a time in the preheated oven for 15 to 20 minutes or until they're golden brown. Let the cookies cool on the baking sheets for 5 minutes. Transfer the cookies to a wire rack to cool completely.

Makes: 32 gems

2 tablespoons chia seeds or flaxseeds

3 tablespoons freshly squeezed orange juice

¼ cup Canna Coco Oil (page 13) or Canna Ghee (page 16)

2 tablespoons liquid honey

⅓ cup finely chopped dried apricots

⅓ cup chopped dried cherries

⅓ cup chopped toasted pecans

3 tablespoons raw sesame seeds

1 teaspoon pure almond extract

1 cup ground almonds

1. Line a baking sheet with parchment paper.

2. Whisk the chia seeds into the orange juice in a small bowl. Set it aside.

3. Combine the Canna Coco Oil, honey, apricots, cherries, pecans, sesame seeds, and almond extract in a food processor and process for 30 seconds. Add the chia mixture and the ground almonds, and pulse 2 or 3 times or until the ingredients are well combined.

4. Scoop out 2 tablespoons of the dough and roll it between the palms of your hands. Arrange the balls in one layer on the prepared baking sheet. Using a lightly oiled fork, gently press the balls to flatten them. Refrigerate the gems on the baking sheet for an hour or until they are firm.

5. Transfer the gems to an airtight container. Seal and label the container, and keep it refrigerated, out of the reach of children.

1 serving = 2 or 3 gems

DOSE: 2 Fruit, Nut, and Seed Gems provide about 4 mg THC and 3 Gems provide about 6 mg THC if you have used the Recommended Carrier Amounts table (page 9) to make the Canna Coco Oil.

STORAGE: Fruit, Nut, and Seed Gems will keep for up to 1 week in an airtight container in the refrigerator.

TO FREEZE: Arrange the Fruit, Nut, and Seed Gems in a single layer on a rimmed baking sheet and freeze them for 30 minutes. Transfer the gems to a resealable bag. Seal and label the bag, and keep it in the freezer for up to 5 months.

Makes: 1 cup

1 trimmed and seeded
jalapeño pepper, optional

1 large clove garlic

1 large tomato, quartered

¼ red onion

1 tablespoon balsamic
vinegar

¼ teaspoon sea salt

1½ cups fresh basil or mint
leaves, lightly packed

About ¼ cup Canna Oil
(page 15)

1 tablespoon extra-virgin
olive oil

6 ounces halloumi or paneer,
cut into equal pieces (see
Recipe Note)

1 serving = 1 tablespoon

DOSE: 1 tablespoon Canna
Basil Chutney provides about
5 mg THC, if you have used
the Recommended Carrier
Amounts table (page 9) to
make the Canna Oil.

STORAGE: Canna Basil
Chutney will keep for up
to 1 week in an airtight
container in the refrigerator.

1. Chop the pepper (if using) and garlic in a small food processor.
   Add the tomato and onion and pulse for 10 seconds. Sprinkle the
   vinegar and salt over the mixture and add the basil to the food
   processor. With the motor running, add the Canna Oil through the
   feed tube. Add just enough oil to make a thick and chunky mixture.
   Scrape into a small bowl and set aside.

2. Heat the olive oil in a grill pan over high heat. Add the halloumi to
   the hot pan and grill for 1 to 2 minutes on each side. Transfer the
   cheese to a serving dish and top with 1 tablespoon of Canna Basil
   Chutney per serving.

Recipe Note

- Halloumi, a Greek specialty, is a semi-hard, unripened sheep's milk
  cheese that does not melt when grilled. While paneer, the Indian-
  style cheese, may also be grilled, in this recipe, the taste and
  texture will be quite different from that of halloumi.

Makes: 12 muffins

1½ cups chopped pitted dates

¾ cup just boiled water

1¾ cups oat or spelt flour

¼ cup ground flaxseeds

2 teaspoons baking powder

2 teaspoons baking soda

2 teaspoons ground cinnamon

1 teaspoon grated fresh ginger or ½ teaspoon ground ginger

1 teaspoon ground nutmeg

½ teaspoon salt

1½ cups grated zucchini or pumpkin

½ cup raisins

½ cup unsalted, hulled sunflower seeds

½ cup Canna Ghee (page 16) or Canna Oil (page 15)

1 tablespoon apple cider vinegar

1. Combine the dates and water in a bowl. Stir the mixture well and cover the bowl with aluminum foil or a pot lid. Set the dates aside for at least 30 minutes to soften.

2. Preheat the oven to 375°F (190°C). Grease a 12-cup muffin pan or use paper liners in the cups.

3. Whisk together the flour, flaxseeds, baking powder, baking soda, cinnamon, ginger, nutmeg, and salt in a large bowl. Stir in the zucchini, raisins, and sunflower seeds.

4. Scrape the dates and soaking water into a food processor, using a rubber spatula, and process for 20 seconds or until the mixture is smooth. Add the Canna Ghee and vinegar, and process for 10 seconds or until the ingredients are well combined. Scrape the mixture into the dry ingredients and stir well.

5. Spoon ¼ cup of batter into each of the prepared muffin cups. Bake the muffins for 23 minutes or until they are lightly browned and a toothpick inserted into the center of a muffin comes out clean.

---

1 serving = 1 muffin

DOSE: 1 Zucchini Muffin provides about 5 mg THC, if you have used the Recommended Carrier Amounts table (page 9) to make the Canna Ghee.

STORAGE: Transfer the cooled muffins to an airtight container. Seal and label the container, and keep it in the refrigerator, out of the reach of children, for up to 1 week.

TO FREEZE: Arrange the muffins in a single layer on a baking sheet and freeze them for 30 minutes. Transfer the muffins to a resealable bag. Seal and label the bag, and keep it in the freezer for up to 4 months.

->>> Zoom Bars

½ cup dried banana chips

½ cup chopped dried apricots

½ cup walnut pieces

½ cup shredded unsweetened coconut

¼ cup large-flake rolled oats

3 tablespoons Canna Nut Butter (page 29)

---

1 serving = 1 bar

DOSE: 1 Zoom Bar provides about 6 mg THC, if you have used the Recommended Carrier Amounts table (page 9) to make the Canna Nut Butter.

STORAGE: Wrap each bar separately in parchment paper and store them in an airtight container at room temperature for up to 1 week or in the refrigerator for up to 2 weeks. Label the container and keep it out of the reach of children.

TO FREEZE: Transfer the individually wrapped bars to a resealable bag. Label the bag and keep it in the freezer for up to 3 months.

1. Line a loaf pan with parchment paper, leaving a 2-inch overhang of paper on the 2 long sides of the pan.

2. Place the banana chips, apricots, walnuts, coconut, rolled oats, and Canna Nut Butter in a food processor and process for 1 minute or until all the ingredients are chopped and completely incorporated. Press the mixture into the prepared pan (use the oiled flat bottom of a drinking glass to tightly pack and smooth the mixture).

3. Cover the pan and refrigerate it for at least 30 minutes or overnight. Using the parchment paper, lift the chilled mixture out of the pan and transfer it to a cutting board. Slice it into 8 equal bars (use a ruler for accuracy).

CANNABIS AT THE SPA

Many herbs, such as calendula, lavender, burdock, rose, chamomile, mint, and dandelion, are known to make you feel and look good. As a "mother herb," with calming, pain-relieving, and skin-soothing properties, Cannabis is also a natural for spa treatments.

Since many terpenes and flavonoids (see Glossary, page 205) are lost in decarboxylation, raw Cannabis contains more healing cannabinoids (in amounts and quality unique to the strain you are using). So in the recipes below that are for topical use such as the Muscle Pain Relief Salve (page 100), you may find that it's more convenient and beneficial to use raw Cannabis. For example, my Nourishing Bath Bomb (page 101) provides therapeutic relief for sore, tired muscles without the extra step of decarboxylating the Cannabis flower. Of course, because it's nonpsychoactive, you won't see a "dose" for topical recipes using raw Cannabis.

Since pain and inflammation are two of the most common ailments treatable at health spas, take a look at "Deflating Inflammation" (page 68) for more information, and try Calming Latte (page 167), Golden Latte (page 169), or Green CBD Smoothie (page 81) while taking a deep soak or massage. And also see the Joint Pain Relief Body Rub (page 73).

You can add other power herbs to any of the following spa recipes, if you are treating a specific condition. See Appendix B (page 186) for suggested ratios and herbs for various conditions.

Muscle Pain Relief Salve

(a raw Cannabis recipe)

1 cup dried arnica aerial parts (see Resources, page 210)

½ cup calendula petals (see Resources, page 210)

½ ounce (14 grams) high-CBD dried raw Cannabis, leaf and/or flower, roughly chopped

3 to 3½ cups melted extra-virgin coconut oil (see Recipe Notes below)

1. Combine the arnica, calendula, and Cannabis in a 1-quart Mason jar. Cover the herbs with oil, leaving 1 or 2 inches of headspace. Loosely screw on the lid and place the jar in a slow cooker lined with a folded tea towel. Add just enough water to reach halfway up the sides of the jar. Cover the slow cooker with the lid (see Recipe Notes below). Turn the heat to low and leave the slow cooker on for 2 days to infuse the oil. Using oven mitts, gently swirl the jar a couple of times a day.

2. Unplug the slow cooker, remove the jar using oven mitts, and set it aside to cool on a wire rack. When the jar is cool enough to handle, strain the infused oil through a layer of cheesecloth, or a basket-style paper coffee filter, into a 3-cup jug or a large liquid measuring cup, allowing the herbs to release all the oil without squeezing or pressing on them. Discard the strained solids. Seal and label the jar, and store it in a cool, dark place, out of the reach of children. (If desired, divide the salve among several small jars.)

Recipe Notes

- Massage the salve into sore muscles or use it on bruises.

- Coconut oil solidifies at temperatures below 76°F (24°C), so if this salve is solid when you are ready to use it, soften it by rubbing a spoonful between the palms of your hands or by placing the jar in a pan of warm water (see how to melt solid coconut oil below). Apply a generous amount of salve directly to your skin, as often as necessary.

- *To melt solid coconut oil:* Set the jar in a saucepan filled with 1 to 2 inches of simmering water. Swirl the jar occasionally until the oil has melted.

- If your jar is too tall to fit comfortably under the lid of your slow cooker in step 1, divide the contents between 2 smaller jars or raise the temperature to keep the water simmering, with the lid off the slow cooker.

- If you don't have a slow cooker, you can simply set the jar of herbs and oil in a sunny window, or another warm spot, and let it steep for 2 weeks or up to 1 month, shaking the jar occasionally.

>>>> CBD-Spiked Relax Spa Scrub

Makes: 2 cups

2 cups coarse
   granulated sugar

40 drops high-CBD oil or
   Canna Oil (page 15)

20 drops rose essential oil

20 drops lavender
   essential oil

STORAGE: CBD-Spiked
Relax Spa Scrub can be kept
in an airtight container for
up to 2 months.

— Combine the sugar, CBD Oil, rose essential oil, and lavender essential oil in a bowl. Stir well. Transfer the mixture to a jar with a lid. Label the jar and store in a cool place, out of the reach of children.

— *To use after a shower or a bath:* Sit on a chair in the bathtub or on the side of the tub facing inward. Place a couple tablespoons of the scrub in the palm of your hand and gently rub it over your body to exfoliate and condition your skin. Start with your feet and ankles and then your legs and thighs. You can also use the mix to scrub your abdomen and work up to your face, neck, shoulders, chest, and down your arms to your hands. Using a towel or a washcloth, lightly brush away any sugar or lightly rinse your skin in lukewarm water, but leave the oils on to penetrate your pores. Doing this at night will help you sleep, so put on an old pair of pajamas or track pants and a T-shirt to protect your sheets from the oil.

→ >>> # Nourishing Bath Bomb

(a raw Cannabis recipe)

Makes: about 4 bombs (each 2 inches in diameter)

1 cup baking soda

½ cup Epsom salt

½ cup cornstarch

½ cup citric acid

¼ cup chopped dried raw
Cannabis stems and leaves

¼ cup dried lavender buds,
optional (see Recipe Notes
below)

1 tablespoon castor oil (see
Recipe Notes below)

1 tablespoon water

1 teaspoon lavender
essential oil (see Recipe
Notes below)

About 5 drops purple food
coloring (see Recipe Notes
below)

1 round, 2-piece aluminum
or silicone mold

STORAGE: Nourishing
Bath Bombs will keep in an
airtight container for up to
1 month.

1. Line a rimmed baking sheet with parchment paper or plastic wrap.

2. Combine baking soda, Epsom salt, cornstarch, citric acid, Cannabis,
   and lavender (if using) in a large bowl, stir well.

3. Combine the castor oil, water, essential oil, and food coloring
   in a jar or small bowl. Shake or mix well and slowly add about a
   teaspoon of the liquid ingredients over the baking soda mixture
   and whisk in. Keep adding liquid ingredients slowly, whisking until
   completely added.

4. Tightly pack the mixture into each half of the round mold and snap
   or screw the halves together. Gently remove the mold and place
   bomb on prepared baking sheet. Set aside to dry for a day. Repeat
   until all of the mixture has been used.

Recipe Notes:

- You can use any combination of herbs, essential oil, and color.
  Here are some variations:
    - Rose petals + rose essential oil + red color
    - Calendula petals + vanilla essential oil + yellow or orange color
    - Rosemary leaves + rosemary or eucalyptus essential oil +
      green color

- Castor oil soothes muscles and softens skin, so it is the best oil for
  a nourishing bath, but you can substitute almond oil or olive oil.

- Use either food coloring or soap coloring, but only a few drops.
  The coloring will not stain porcelain.

- If you have loose mixture left over, save it and toss into your
  bath water.

Performance Elixir Tincture

Makes: 3 cups

¼ ounce (7 grams) chopped activated Cannabis (page 8; see Recipe Notes below)

½ cup chopped berries (fresh or frozen blueberries, blackberries, strawberries, cherries, raspberries)

¼ cup chopped hawthorn berries, leaves, and flowers, fresh or dried (see Resources, page 210)

1 orange, rind on, sliced

3 tablespoons chopped rose hips, fresh or dried

2 tablespoons Siberian ginseng (or another adaptogen), optional (see Herbs for Enhanced Athletic Performance, page 191, for information about adaptogens)

1 tablespoon grated fresh ginger

1 stick (2 inches) cinnamon

3 cups or more brandy or vodka (40% to 45% alcohol)

2 to 4 tablespoons liquid honey or maple syrup, to taste, optional

1. Combine the Cannabis, berries, hawthorn, orange slices, rose hips, ginseng (if using), ginger, and cinnamon in a wide-mouth quart jar. Add the brandy to the jar, making sure it covers the ingredients. Seal, label, and store the jar at room temperature, away from direct sunlight and heat, and out of the reach of children, for 1 month, shaking the jar once a day or every few days, whenever you remember.

2. Line a fine-mesh strainer with 2 layers of cheesecloth or a basket-style paper coffee filter and set it over a large measuring cup or bowl. Pour the tincture from the jar through the strainer into the measuring cup. Let the oil drip through without squeezing or pressing on the filter. Discard the solids.

3. Taste the tincture and stir in honey to taste. Pour the elixir into a jar with a lid. Label and store the jar in a cool, dark cupboard, out of the reach of children. Take a dose just prior to eating.

DOSE: 1 teaspoon or 20 drops of Performance Elixir Tincture will provide about 5 mg THC, if you use a strain of Cannabis that is between 10% and 12% THC and 3 cups of brandy. The dose of 1 teaspoon will provide slightly less THC (about 4 mg) if you use 3½ cups brandy with the same percentage of THC.

STORAGE: Alcohol and vinegar tinctures will keep for years at a cool room temperature or in the refrigerator.

Recipe Note

- Use a sativa strain with 10% to 12% THC, if possible.

(a raw Cannabis recipe)

Makes: 2 packs, no THC

3 tablespoons dried
lavender buds

3 tablespoons large-flake
rolled oats

2 tablespoons high-CBD
raw Cannabis, coarsely
chopped (see Recipe Notes
below)

2 tablespoons dried
rosemary

2 pieces (6 inches square)
muslin or doubled
cheesecloth (4 layers,
see Recipe Notes below)

2 pieces (8 inches each)
kitchen twine

½ cup cold-pressed
almond oil

2 teaspoons coconut oil

1. Combine the lavender, oatmeal, Cannabis, and rosemary in a small bowl and mix well. Divide the mixture into 2 equal portions and place a portion in the center of each muslin square. Gather the corners and edges of each square together to form a pouch around the herbs and tie it with twine.

2. Combine the almond oil and coconut oil in the top of a double boiler and heat over simmering water until it is warmed but not too hot. Leave the oil in the top pan over the hot water with the heat turned off.

3. Place both pouches (poultice packs) in the oil and let them sit until they are fully saturated (about 10 minutes).

— *To massage aching muscles:* Use one poultice pack at a time, leaving the other pack in the warming oil. Massage bruised or achy muscles in a gentle, circular motion. When the pack cools, replace it in the oil and use the warmed pack. Turn the heat on under the bottom double-boiler pan if the oil cools down. Massage for at least 20 minutes.

Recipe Notes

- Use chopped raw Cannabis leaves, soft stems, and flowers in the poultice.

- Clean muslin or squares cut from old cotton or linen sheets may be used. If you are using cheesecloth, it usually comes folded, automatically providing 2 layers. When you fold it before cutting, you create 4 layers in each square. An all-purpose size of 6 square inches is given, however, you can cut the square to fit the area you are treating.

CHAPTER 4

< Light Main Meals >

It may seem that the recipes in this section are a little, well . . . somewhat on the light side—more like appetizers than anything else. In fact, that's what they are. Unless you are serving Cannabis edibles to like-minded adults in a recreational mood, it's not appropriate to add Cannabis to pork chops or heartier dishes, such as soups or stews, whole chicken, roasts, and other foods. These kinds of dishes make it difficult to control the dose of THC per serving, and it assumes that everyone will want to partake.

You can always add a serving of a spice paste or spread, such as those in chapter 1 (beginning on page 1); sauces such as Canna Churri (page 45) and Chile Tapenade (page 89); or Canna Basil Chutney (page 93) to roasted or grilled meats, vegetables, and cooked pasta. By sidelining the Cannabis to condiments, people who do not wish to consume Cannabis have the option to not add it to their food.

With some exceptions, the recipes in this section are plant-forward, single-serve foods for lunch, dinner, or in-between. If you want to make a whole meal of a dish, make a batch without Cannabis so that you can supplement the smaller, 5 mg Cannabis serving with Cannabis-free, entrée-size portions.

< 105 >

>>>> Baked Chicken Wings with Canna Hot Sauce

Makes: 12 wings, no THC

3 tablespoons extra-virgin avocado oil or olive oil

4 cloves garlic, minced

3 tablespoons tamari or soy sauce

2 tablespoons liquid honey

12 chicken wings, skin on

Canna Hot Sauce (recipe follows)

1. Combine the oil, garlic, tamari, and honey in a large resealable bag. Seal and shake the bag to combine the marinade mixture. Add the chicken wings to the bag and massage the wings to coat them with the mixture. Refrigerate the wings for at least 30 minutes or overnight to marinate.

2. Meanwhile, preheat the oven to 375°F (190°C). Line a rimmed baking sheet with parchment paper and place a rack on top of the paper.

3. Arrange the chicken wings in a layer on the rack. Drizzle the wings with any leftover marinade from the bag. Bake the wings in the preheated oven for 1 hour. The wings should be crisp and are done when they reach an internal temperature of 165°F (74°C). Serve the wings with ½ cup Canna Hot Sauce per serving as desired.

CANNA HOT SAUCE

Makes: 2¼ cups

1 can (19 ounces) or 2 cups fresh diced tomatoes, drained

2 tablespoons Canna Honey (page 24)

½ onion, finely chopped

2 teaspoons ground oregano

2 teaspoons ground chile seasoning, or to taste

— Combine the tomatoes, Canna Honey, onion, oregano, and chile in a food processor or blender and pulse 2 or 3 times or until blended.

1 serving = ½ cup

DOSE: ½ cup Canna Hot Sauce provides about 6 mg THC, if you have used the Recommended Carrier Amounts table (page 9) to make the Canna Honey.

STORAGE: If you make 2 servings of wings and serve ½ cup of Canna Hot Sauce per serving, you will have just over 1 cup of sauce left. The sauce will keep in an airtight container in the refrigerator for up to 1 week.

TO FREEZE: Divide the remaining sauce into ½-cup portions and transfer them to 2 freezer containers or resealable bags. Seal, label, and freeze the bags for up to 5 months. Thaw the sauce in the refrigerator overnight before using.

Asparagus-Stuffed Mushrooms

Makes: 12 mushrooms

12 large cremini or small
portobello mushrooms

3 tablespoons extra-virgin
olive oil, divided (see
Recipe Notes opposite)

½ onion, finely chopped

10 asparagus spears,
trimmed and cut into
½-inch pieces

1 clove garlic, finely
chopped

¼ cup salted sunflower seeds

1 tablespoon balsamic
vinegar

1 teaspoon Canna Oil
(page 15) per serving (see
Recipe Notes opposite)

1. Preheat the oven to 375°F (190°C). Line a rimmed baking sheet with parchment paper.

2. Rinse and wipe the mushrooms with a dry towel. Remove the stems, chop them, and set aside. Arrange the caps, gill-sides down, on the prepared baking sheet. Brush with 1 tablespoon of the olive oil and bake in the preheated oven for 15 minutes.

3. Meanwhile, prepare the filling: Heat the remaining olive oil in a skillet over medium-high heat. Add the chopped mushroom stems, onions, asparagus, and garlic. Cook, stirring frequently, for 6 minutes or until the asparagus offers slight resistance when tested with the tip of a knife. The mixture should be fairly dry. Remove the skillet from the stove and stir in the sunflower seeds and vinegar.

4. Remove the baking sheet and flip the mushrooms, using tongs, so they're gill-side up. Divide the filling into 12 equal portions and stuff into each cap. Return to the oven and bake for 10 minutes or until the mushrooms are tender and the stuffing is bubbling.

5. Drizzle 1 stuffed mushroom with 1 teaspoon Canna Oil and enjoy. Let the remaining mushrooms cool completely before storing (see opposite).

1 serving = see Recipe Notes

DOSE: 1 teaspoon Canna Oil added to 1 Asparagus-Stuffed Mushroom provides about 5 mg THC if you have used the Recommended Carrier Amounts table (page 9) to make the Canna Oil.

STORAGE: Transfer stuffed mushrooms to an airtight container, label, and keep in the refrigerator for up to 4 days.

TO FREEZE: Wrap mushrooms individually in foil, transfer to a resealable bag, and freeze for up to 3 months.

TO REHEAT: Place each foil-wrapped mushroom in the refrigerator overnight to thaw and heat in the foil at 325°F (160°C) for 10 minutes or until warm.

Recipe Notes

- Since you are only adding 1 dose (1 teaspoon) of Canna Oil to one mushroom, you can consume as many as you wish because the remaining mushrooms do not contain Cannabis.

- An alternative way to add Cannabis to each mushroom in the recipe is to substitute ¼ cup Canna Oil for the 3 tablespoons of extra-virgin olive oil. Of course, since each of these Asparagus-Stuffed Mushrooms would then be infused with Cannabis, *take only one stuffed mushroom at a sitting and do not add the 1 teaspoon of Canna Oil* at the end.

>>>> Baked Tomato-Garlic Chicken Drumsticks with Canna Tzatziki Sauce

Makes: 12 drumsticks, no THC

1 tablespoon freshly squeezed lemon juice

1 tablespoon fresh thyme leaves or chopped fresh rosemary

Sea salt and pepper, to taste

12 chicken drumsticks, skin intact

¼ cup tomato paste

1 tablespoon extra-virgin avocado oil or olive oil

1 tablespoon commercial hot sauce, optional

¼ cup shredded Parmesan cheese

1 cup Canna Tzatziki Sauce (recipe follows)

1. Preheat the oven to 375°F (190°C). Line a rimmed baking sheet with foil and place a wire rack on the foil.

2. Combine the lemon juice, thyme, and salt and pepper in a large, resealable bag. Add the drumsticks, seal the bag, and massage the drumsticks to coat them evenly. Arrange the drumsticks on the prepared baking rack and bake them in the preheated oven for 20 minutes (the drumsticks won't be fully cooked yet).

3. Meanwhile, combine the tomato paste, oil, and hot sauce (if using) in a small bowl.

4. Baste the partially cooked drumsticks with the tomato mixture. Sprinkle them with cheese and put them back in the oven. Bake the drumsticks for an additional 12 to 17 minutes or until the outside is crisp and the meat registers 165°F (74°C) on a meat thermometer. Serve with the sauce.

CANNA TZATZIKI SAUCE

Makes: 1 cup

1 cup shredded cucumber

½ cup Greek-style whole milk yogurt

1 tablespoon Canna Oil (page 15)

2 cloves garlic, minced

1 teaspoon finely grated lemon zest

2 tablespoons freshly squeezed lemon juice

1 tablespoon chopped fresh dill, optional

Sea salt and pepper, to taste

---

1 serving = ¼ cup

DOSE: ¼ cup Canna Tzatziki Sauce provides about 4 mg THC, if you have used the Recommended Carrier Amounts table (page 9) to make the Canna Oil.

STORAGE: If you use ¼ cup Canna Tzatziki Sauce per serving, you could have ¾ cup, or 3 servings, left over. Keep Canna Tzatziki Sauce in an airtight container in the refrigerator, out of the reach of children, for up to 1 week. This sauce does not freeze well.

1. Place the shredded cucumber in a colander over the sink and let it drain for 10 to 15 minutes. Press down on the cucumber to release excess moisture and then transfer it to a large bowl. Add the yogurt and Canna Oil and stir well. Add the garlic, lemon zest and juice, and dill (if using). Stir well. Season with salt and pepper.

2. Serve the sauce with Baked Tomato-Garlic Chicken Drumsticks (opposite page); non-Cannabis Moroccan Meatballs (page 128); or Baked Chicken Wings (page 107).

>>>> Baked Vegetable Chips with Canna Salsa

Makes: 2 servings, no THC

1 sweet potato, sliced crosswise into ⅛-inch rounds

1 large beet, sliced crosswise into ⅛-inch rounds

2 tablespoons extra-virgin olive oil or avocado oil

1 tablespoon crushed cumin seeds

½ teaspoon kosher salt, plus more for serving

1 batch Canna Salsa (recipe follows) or Canna Roasted Red Pepper Hummus (page 88)

STORAGE: Baked Vegetable Chips are best eaten warm right out of the oven. Store leftovers in a resealable, airtight bag or container in the refrigerator for up to 3 days.

1. Preheat the oven to 400°F (200°C). Line a rimmed baking sheet with parchment paper.

2. Toss together the sweet potato and beet slices, oil, cumin, and salt in a bowl. Spread the ingredients on the prepared baking sheet in a single layer and bake them in the preheated oven for 20 minutes. Stir and bake the vegetable chips for an additional 10 minutes or until they're crisp on the outside and tender on the inside when pierced with a sharp knife. Taste and sprinkle the chips with salt, if desired, and serve them warm with Canna Salsa.

Recipe Note

- Children love vegetable chips, and they can enjoy them as long as the salsa or hummus they use as a dip is Cannabis-free. Make a couple of batches of the salsa and/or the hummus—one with and one without Cannabis. Be sure to clearly label each of the batches.

CANNA SALSA

2 tablespoons Canna Oil (page 15) or Canna Coco Oil (page 13)

2 tablespoons balsamic vinegar

1 tablespoon coconut sugar

1 teaspoon adobo sauce, optional (see Recipe Note below)

1 clove garlic, minced

1 can (28 ounces) diced tomatoes, drained

½ onion, finely chopped

1 canned chipotle pepper, finely chopped

½ cup chopped fresh cilantro, optional

1. Combine the Canna Oil, vinegar, sugar, adobo sauce (if using), and garlic in a food processor. Pulse the mixture a couple of times until the garlic is finely chopped and all the ingredients are well combined.

2. Transfer the mixture to a bowl. Add the tomatoes, onion, pepper, and cilantro (if using) and stir well to combine.

1 serving = ½ cup

DOSE: ½ cup Canna Salsa provides about 6 mg THC, if you have used the Recommended Carrier Amounts table (page 9) to make the Canna Oil.

STORAGE: If you make 1 batch of Baked Vegetable Chips, this Canna Salsa recipe makes 2 servings. If you serve ½ cup Canna Salsa with each serving of chips, you will have 1 cup of salsa left over. Canna Salsa will keep in the refrigerator in an airtight container for up to 1 week.

TO FREEZE: Divide the remaining salsa into ½-cup portions and place them in resealable bags or freezer containers. Seal, label, and freeze the salsa for up to 5 months. Thaw it in the refrigerator overnight before using it.

Recipe Note

- Roasted chipotle peppers are often packed in a rich paprika sauce called adobo.

>>>> Black Bean Burgers

2 tablespoons extra-virgin coconut oil

1 onion, chopped

4 cups chopped mushrooms

2 cloves garlic, finely chopped

2 tablespoons Canna Nut Butter (page 29) or Canna Oil (page 15)

1 can (15 ounces) black beans, rinsed and drained

1 avocado, peeled and pitted

1 cup finely chopped walnuts

1 cup large-flake rolled oats or spelt

6 hamburger buns or lettuce cups (see Recipe Note opposite)

1. Preheat the oven to 350°F (180°C). Line a rimmed baking sheet with parchment paper.

2. Heat the oil in a skillet over medium-high heat. Add the onions and cook, stirring occasionally, for 5 minutes. Add the mushrooms and garlic. Reduce the heat to medium and cook the mixture, stirring frequently, for 12 minutes or until the vegetables are tender (the mixture should be moist with no excess liquid from the mushrooms in the pan). Stir in the Canna Nut Butter and set the pan aside.

3. Meanwhile mash the beans and avocado using a potato masher or blend them in a food processor (the consistency should be smooth and paste-like, with the occasional whole bean throughout).

4. Combine the mushroom mixture, bean and avocado mixture, walnuts, and oats in a large bowl. Pack the mixture into a ½-cup measure, using a small spatula or the back of a spoon to press it in firmly and level the top with a knife. Invert the cup over the baking sheet and use the spatula to ease the mixture onto the baking sheet. Gently press the mixture into a patty that is at least 1½ inches high. Repeat until all the remaining mixture is used.

5. Bake the patties in the preheated oven for 30 minutes or until they're firm. Let the patties rest for 7 minutes before serving.

1 serving = 1 patty

DOSE: 1 Black Bean Burger provides about 5 mg THC, if you have used the Recommended Carrier Amounts table (page 9) to make the Canna Nut Butter.

STORAGE: Store tightly wrapped patties in the refrigerator, out of the reach of children, for up to 5 days.

TO FREEZE: Wrap the cooked patties individually in foil, label them, place them in a resealable bag, and keep them frozen for up to 3 months.

TO REHEAT: Heat frozen patties in the foil at 325°F (160°C) for 20 minutes or until warm.

Recipe Note

- Serve the patties in a bun and garnish them, if desired, with non-Cannabis sauce and other condiments. You can also wrap the patties in lettuce cups and serve them with Cannabis Leaf Pesto (page 49), Peanut Sauce (page 123), or other non-Cannabis condiments.

Makes: 10 to 12 tots

2 cups broccoli florets or roughly chopped kale

½ onion, roughly chopped

½ cup roughly chopped walnuts

3 tablespoons Sweet Canna Thai Spice Paste (page 43)

1 large egg

1. Preheat the oven to 375°F (190°C). Line a rimmed baking sheet with parchment paper.

2. Bring a saucepan of salted water to a boil. Add the broccoli florets and cook them for 3 minutes. Drain and rinse the florets under cold running water to stop them from cooking and pat them dry. Set the florets aside. (The same instructions apply to chopped kale.)

3. Combine the onions, walnuts, and Sweet Canna Thai Spice Paste in a food processor and pulse 3 or 4 times. Add the broccoli and pulse a couple times to mix well. With the motor running, add the egg and process for 10 seconds or until the mixture is finely chopped.

4. Scoop 2 tablespoons of the mixture into the palm of your hand. Gently shape it into the form of a tater tot and place it on the prepared baking sheet. Repeat until the entire mixture has been used up.

5. Bake the Broccoli Tots in the preheated oven for 20 minutes or until they're crisp on the outside and lightly browned.

1 serving = 1 tot

DOSE: 1 Broccoli Tot provides about 4 mg THC, if you have used the Recommended Carrier Amounts table (page 9) to make the Sweet Canna Thai Spice Paste.

STORAGE: Let the Broccoli Tots cool completely, and then transfer them to an airtight container. Label and refrigerate the container, out of the reach of children, for up to 4 days.

TO FREEZE: Arrange the tots in a single layer on a parchment-lined rimmed baking sheet and freeze them for 30 minutes. Transfer the tots to a resealable bag. Label the bag and keep it in the freezer for up to 3 months.

TO REHEAT: Preheat the oven to 350°F (180°C). Arrange the frozen tots in a single layer on a baking sheet and bake them for 7 to 12 minutes or until they're heated through.

>>> Canna Guacamole

1 tablespoon Canna Oil
(page 15; see Recipe Notes
below)

Juice of 1 lemon

2 cloves garlic, minced

¼ teaspoon sea salt

1 teaspoon ground cayenne
pepper, optional

3 avocados

---

1 serving = ½ cup

DOSE: ½ cup Canna
Guacamole provides about
4 mg THC, if you have used
the Recommended Carrier
Amounts table (page 9) to
make Canna Oil.

STORAGE: It's best to
use Canna Guacamole
immediately, but it will
keep in the refrigerator for
up to 3 days, if it is well
covered.

---

1. Combine the Canna Oil, lemon juice, garlic, salt, and cayenne pepper (if using) in a food processor. Pulse to mix.

2. Peel, pit, and slice 1 avocado and add it to the Canna Oil mixture in the food processor. Pulse 3 or 4 times to blend the ingredients. Repeat with the remaining avocados. Transfer the mixture to a bowl.

Recipe Notes

- If you are using high-CBD and very low-THC oil, you can use a larger amount of Canna Oil. Be sure to label any Cannabis food you store, and keep it out of the reach of children.

- You can add Canna Guacamole to smoothies and scrambled eggs; use it as a dip for vegetables or nachos or as a spread for wraps and burritos, or substitute it for mayonnaise in salad. Just be mindful of the amount you ingest at any one time, and don't add Canna Guacamole to a dish that is already infused with Cannabis.

Canna Chicken-Stuffed Peppers

Makes: 4 peppers

4 red bell peppers

¼ cup mayonnaise

2 tablespoons Canna Oil
(page 15)

1½ cups cooked, chopped
chicken

1 cup chopped kale or
spinach

½ cup cooked quinoa,
steel-cut oats, or wild rice

½ cup chopped feta cheese
or shredded Cheddar
cheese

1 serving = 1 pepper

DOSE: 1 Chicken-Stuffed
Pepper provides about
6 mg THC, if you have used
the Recommended Carrier
Amounts table (page 9)
to make the Canna Oil.

STORAGE: Transfer the
peppers to an airtight
container. Label the
container and keep it in
the refrigerator, out of the
reach of children, for up to
5 days.

1. Preheat the oven to 350°F (180°C). Line a baking sheet with
   parchment paper.

2. Run a paring knife around the stem of each pepper and remove and
   discard it, keeping the peppers whole. Thinly slice the bottom of
   each pepper, if necessary, to allow the peppers to stand upright.
   Scoop out the ribs and seeds and discard them. Arrange the
   peppers upright on the baking sheet.

3. Combine the mayonnaise and Canna Oil in a large bowl. Add the
   chicken, kale, quinoa, and cheese and stir well. Divide the mixture
   to evenly fill each of the peppers.

4. Bake the peppers for 12 to 15 minutes or until they offer slight
   resistance when pierced with the tip of a sharp knife.

Egg and Shiitake Mushroom Popovers

¼ cup Canna Ghee (page 16) or Canna Coco Oil (page 13)

1 onion, chopped

1 cup finely chopped shiitake mushrooms

½ cup chopped spinach, fresh, or thawed and drained, if frozen

1 large tomato, chopped

6 large eggs

2 tablespoons milk

½ teaspoon sea salt

1. Preheat the oven to 350°F (180°C). Line a 12-cup muffin pan with paper cups or lightly oil the pan.

2. Place the Canna Ghee in a large skillet over medium-high heat. Add the onion and mushrooms and cook, stirring frequently, for 5 minutes or until the vegetables are soft. Add the spinach and cook, stirring frequently, for 1 minute or until the leaves have wilted. Remove the skillet from the stove, stir in the tomato, and set the pan aside to cool for at least 10 minutes.

3. Meanwhile, whisk together the eggs, milk, and salt in a large bowl. Add the sautéed vegetables and stir using a fork, until the ingredients are evenly incorporated.

4. Fill each muffin well with ¼ cup batter. Bake the popovers in the preheated oven for 12 to 15 minutes or until they are browned and firm. Enjoy them warm or cold.

1 serving = 1 popover

DOSE: 1 Egg and Shiitake Mushroom Popover provides about 5 mg THC, if you have used the Recommended Carrier Amounts table (page 9) to make the Canna Ghee.

STORAGE: Let the popovers cool completely in the pan. Transfer them to an airtight container and refrigerate them for up to 4 days, out of the reach of children.

TO FREEZE: Wrap cooled popovers individually in foil. Transfer them to a resealable bag and freeze for up to 3 months.

TO REHEAT: Thaw the popovers in the refrigerator overnight (in their foil wrapping) and place them, still in their foil wrapping, in a preheated 325°F (160°C) oven for 10 minutes or until warm.

>>>> Falafel with Peanut Sauce

1 cup dried chickpeas, soaked in water overnight and drained (see Recipe Notes below)

1 onion, finely chopped

3 tablespoons Canna Curry Spice Paste (page 41; see Recipe Notes below)

2 tablespoons chopped fresh parsley, optional

Extra-virgin avocado or coconut oil, for frying

---

1 serving = 1 falafel

DOSE: 1 Falafel provides about 6 mg THC, if you have used the Recommended Carrier Amounts table (page 9) to make the Canna Curry Spice Paste.

---

1. Line a baking sheet with parchment paper. Line a second baking sheet or large platter with paper towels.

2. Drain the chickpeas and combine them with the onion, Canna Curry Spice Paste, and parsley (if using) in a food processor. Process for 30 seconds or until the ingredients are well mixed.

3. Measure 2 tablespoons of the mixture and shape it into a patty. Place it on the prepared baking sheet. Repeat with the remaining mixture.

4. Pour about 1 inch of oil into a large, deep skillet over medium-high heat. Working in batches, cook the falafel patties for about 5 minutes, turning them once or twice, until they're crisp and golden all over. Using tongs, transfer the patties to a paper towel–lined platter and let the patties drain.

Recipe Notes

- Making falafel with soaked dried chickpeas ensures that they will not fall apart during cooking. I recommend that you do not use canned chickpeas.

- If you don't have Canna Curry Spice Paste, use 3 tablespoons Canna Coco Oil (page 13) or Canna Oil (page 15), and add 1 minced clove garlic, 1 teaspoon ground cumin, 1 teaspoon ground coriander, and ½ teaspoon ground cinnamon to the food processor in step 2.

PEANUT SAUCE

Makes: ½ cup, no THC

½ cup peanut butter

3 tablespoons coconut milk

Juice of ½ lime

¼ teaspoon dried chile flakes, optional

— Combine the peanut butter, milk, lime juice, and chile flakes (if using) in a bowl and stir well.

— **To make a Cannabis-infused Peanut Sauce:** First double the recipe to make 1 cup Canna Peanut Sauce. Add 1 tablespoon Canna Nut Butter (page 29) or Spiced Canna Nut Butter (page 31) to the 1 cup regular peanut butter and double all other ingredients. Be sure to label and store the sauce out of the reach of children. If you are using a Cannabis-infused Peanut Sauce, do not use Canna Curry Spice Paste in the Falafel. Instead use 1 tablespoon (or to taste) regular powdered curry.

>>> Goat Cheese and Onion Tart

Makes: 1 tart, 9 x 9 inches

3 tablespoons extra-virgin olive oil

2 large onions, thinly sliced (4 cups)

2 large cloves garlic, slivered

3 tablespoons white wine or white wine vinegar

4 sprigs fresh thyme, leaves stripped, stems discarded

1 roll puff pastry, thawed (see Recipe Notes opposite)

8 to 12 artichoke hearts, drained (see Recipe Notes opposite)

½ cup walnuts

4½ ounces soft goat cheese

¼ cup Canna Coco Oil (page 13)

1 tablespoon freshly squeezed lemon juice

Sea salt and pepper

1. Preheat the oven to 425° F (220° C) and line a rimmed baking sheet with parchment paper.

2. Heat the olive oil in a large skillet over medium-low heat. Add the onions and garlic and sauté for 5 minutes. Cover, reduce heat to low, and sweat the onions for 15 to 20 minutes or until they are limp. Add the wine and thyme, cover, and continue to cook, stirring occasionally, for 10 minutes or until the onions are a light golden color and the liquid has evaporated. Set the pan aside to cool slightly.

3. Meanwhile, unroll 1 sheet of puff pastry and spread it out on the prepared baking sheet. Using the tip of a paring knife, score the inside perimeter of the dough, ½ inch from the edge of the pastry (see Recipe Notes).

4. Combine the artichoke hearts, walnuts, cheese, Canna Coco Oil, and lemon juice in a food processor. Pulse for 30 seconds or until the ingredients are well blended. Add salt and pepper to taste. Spread the mixture on the puff pastry inside the ½-inch border. Spread the onion mixture over the cheese mixture, staying within the ½-inch border. Bake the pastry in the preheated oven for 20 to 25 minutes or until it is puffed and golden brown.

5. Let the tart rest for 5 minutes before serving. Use a ruler to cut 9 pieces that measure 3 inches square.

1 serving = 1 square
(3 x 3-inches), see Recipe
Notes

DOSE: 1 Goat Cheese
and Onion square
(3 x 3 inches) provides
about 5 mg THC, if you have
used the Recommended
Carrier Amounts table
(page 9) to make the Canna
Coco Oil.

Recipe Notes

- Puff pastry may be found in the freezer section of the supermarket. Usually, 1 box contains 2 rolls. For this amount of filling, use 1 roll and thaw it overnight in the refrigerator before using it.

- Scoring around the perimeter of the dough, as described in step 3, allows for the formation of a rim when the dough bakes. You can also create a rim by brushing the perimeter edges with melted butter and rolling the edges over about ¼ inch. Either method works to form a bit of a raised edge to hold the filling.

- Artichoke hearts are available packed in oil or water. For this dish, I prefer to use oil-packed artichoke hearts, but either will work. Look for glass jars, rather than cans, if possible.

Mac and Cheese Minis

Makes: 12 minis

1 cup dried macaroni, regular or gluten-free

1½ cups chopped cabbage or cauliflower

¼ cup Canna Ghee (page 16) or Canna Oil (page 15)

3 tablespoons all-purpose flour or gluten-free flour blend

1¼ cups milk

½ teaspoon salt

½ teaspoon mustard powder, optional

2 cups shredded sharp Cheddar cheese

½ cup panko breadcrumbs

½ cup grated Parmesan cheese

1 tablespoon extra-virgin olive oil

1. Preheat the oven to 425°F (220°C). Line or lightly oil a 12-cup muffin pan.

2. Bring a large saucepan of salted water to a boil. Add the macaroni and cook for 5 minutes. Add the cabbage and cook until the macaroni is al dente and the cabbage is crisp-tender when pierced with the tip of a sharp knife. Drain the macaroni and cabbage in a colander and set it aside, reserving the saucepan.

3. In the reserved saucepan, heat the Canna Ghee over medium-high heat. Add the flour and cook, stirring constantly, for 2 minutes or until a thick paste forms. Whisk in the milk, salt, and mustard powder (if using). Cook the mixture, whisking constantly, for 4 minutes or until it has thickened. Add the Cheddar cheese and stir until it has melted. Add the cabbage and macaroni to the cheese sauce and mix well. Spoon the mixture evenly into the prepared muffin pan.

4. Combine the breadcrumbs, Parmesan cheese, and olive oil in a small bowl. Spoon the mixture evenly over the macaroni and cabbage mixture in the muffin pan. Bake the mac and cheese in the preheated oven for 18 minutes or until the breadcrumb mixture is golden brown and the macaroni mixture is bubbling. Remove the mac and cheese from the oven and let it rest for 5 minutes before serving.

1 serving = 1 mini

DOSE: 1 Mac and Cheese Mini provides about 5 mg THC, if you have used the Recommended Carrier Amounts table (page 9) to make the Canna Ghee.

STORAGE: Keep the Mac and Cheese Minis in an airtight container, out of the reach of children, in the refrigerator for up to 3 days.

TO FREEZE: Arrange the minis in a single layer on a rimmed baking sheet and freeze for 15 minutes. Wrap the minis individually in plastic wrap and place them in a resealable bag or container in the freezer for up to 2 months.

TO REHEAT: Preheat the oven to 350°F (180°C). Remove the plastic wrap from each frozen mini, place the minis in a heatproof pan, and bake them for 35 minutes or until they're golden and heated through.

>>> Moroccan Meatballs

Makes: 24 meatballs

2 tablespoons extra-virgin olive oil or avocado oil

1 onion, finely chopped

1 clove garlic, minced

1 pound minced lamb, chicken, or beef

1 large egg

1 cup cooked quinoa or steel-cut oats

¼ cup finely chopped almonds

3 tablespoons Sweet Canna Thai Spice Paste (page 43)

1. Line a rimmed baking sheet with parchment paper. Preheat the oven to 350°F (180°C).

2. Heat the oil in a skillet over medium-high heat. Add the onion and cook, stirring frequently, for 5 minutes. Add the garlic and cook, stirring frequently, for 2 minutes or until the garlic is fragrant. Remove the pan from the heat and set it aside to cool.

3. Combine the lamb, egg, quinoa, and almonds in a large bowl and stir well. Scrape the onion mixture and juices over the the lamb mixture and stir well. Add the Sweet Canna Thai Spice Paste and stir well.

4. Measure 2 tablespoons of the mixture and roll it between the palms of your hands to form a ball. Place the ball on the prepared baking sheet. Repeat until the entire mixture has been used up.

5. Bake the meatballs in the preheated oven for 12 minutes or until they are no longer pink inside and cooked through (test a meatball by cutting it in half). Serve 1 or 2 meatballs as a between-meal snack or with the main meal at lunch or dinner.

---

1 serving = 2 meatballs

DOSE: 2 Moroccan Meatballs provide about 5 mg THC if you have used the Recommended Carrier Amounts table (page 9) to make the Sweet Canna Thai Spice Paste.

STORAGE: Keep the meatballs in an airtight container in the refrigerator, out of the reach of children, for up to 4 days.

TO FREEZE: Arrange the meatballs in a single layer on parchment-lined rimmed baking sheet and freeze them for 30 minutes. Transfer the meatballs to a resealable bag or container. Seal and label the container, and keep it in the freezer for up to 3 months.

TO REHEAT: Preheat the oven to 350°F (180°C). Place the frozen meatballs on a baking sheet and bake for 7 to 12 minutes or until the meat is heated through.

Recipe Note

- ***To make half Cannabis and half non-Cannabis meatballs:*** Divide the ingredients in half to make 2 batches (use 1 egg per batch). Half of ¼ cup is 2 tablespoons. Cook the non-Canna mixture first, and then the Canna mixture. Roll and drop the meatballs on 2 separate parchment-lined rimmed baking sheets. With a marker, label the Canna baking sheet with a "C." Serve, label, and store the Canna meatballs separately from the non-Canna meatballs.

>>>> Quinoa Salmon Cakes

Makes: 4 cakes

3 tablespoons extra-virgin olive oil, divided

½ onion, chopped

6 mushrooms, sliced

2 cloves garlic, finely chopped

½ avocado, roughly chopped

Juice of ½ lemon

1 tablespoon Canna Oil (page 15)

1 cup cooked quinoa

½ cup roughly chopped mixed dark greens (kale, mustard, chard, spinach, bok choy)

1 egg, slightly beaten

1 can (5 ounces) wild salmon, drained

Sea salt and pepper, to taste

1. Line a baking sheet with parchment paper.

2. Heat 2 tablespoons of the olive oil in a skillet over medium heat. Add the onions, mushrooms, and garlic and cook, stirring frequently, for 5 minutes or until the vegetables are tender when pierced with the tip of a knife. Remove the pan from the heat and set it aside to cool.

3. In a large bowl, mash together the avocado, lemon juice, and Canna Oil. Add the quinoa, greens, and egg to the bowl and mix well. Stir in the salmon and the onion mixture and toss to mix well. Using slightly wet hands, divide the mixture into 4 even portions. Shape each portion into a round cake about 2 inches thick. Arrange the cakes in a single layer on the prepared baking sheet, season the cakes with salt and pepper, and refrigerate them for 15 minutes. At this point, the cakes can be frozen, if desired (see Storage below).

4. Heat the remaining tablespoon of olive oil in a large skillet over medium heat. Add the cakes and sear them for 5 minutes on each side or until they're browned.

---

1 serving = 1 cake

DOSE: 1 Quinoa Salmon Cake provides about 4 mg THC, if you have used the Recommended Carrier Amounts table (page 9) to make the Canna Oil.

STORAGE: Quinoa Salmon Cakes will keep in an airtight container in the refrigerator for up to 3 days.

TO FREEZE: Omit step 4. Arrange the cakes in a single layer on a rimmed baking sheet and freeze them for 15 minutes. Wrap the cakes individually in plastic wrap and place them in a labeled resealable bag or container. Freeze the cakes for up to 3 months.

TO COOK FROZEN CAKES: Preheat the oven to 350°F (180°C). Remove the plastic wrap, place the patties in a heatproof dish, and bake them for 35 minutes or until they're golden and heated through.

>>>> Spinach Artichoke Bites

Makes: 12 bites

¼ cup **Canna Ghee** (page 16)
or **Canna Coco Oil** (page 13)

1 cup roughly chopped
spinach or kale

½ cup cooked turkey
sausage slices, optional

½ cup chopped artichoke
or zucchini

6 large eggs

2 tablespoons milk

½ teaspoon sea salt

¼ cup shredded
Cheddar cheese

1. Preheat the oven to 350°F (180°C). Grease a 12-cup muffin pan or use paper liners.

2. Heat the Canna Ghee in a large skillet over medium-high heat. Add the spinach and cook, stirring frequently, for 1 minute or until the leaves have wilted. Remove the skillet from the heat, stir in the sausage (if using) and artichoke, and set it aside for at least 10 minutes to cool.

3. Whisk together eggs, milk, and salt in a large bowl. Add the cooled spinach mixture to the bowl and, using a fork, stir until all the ingredients are evenly incorporated.

4. Fill each muffin cup with ¼ cup of the mixture, sprinkle the cheese on top, and bake in the preheated oven for 12 to 15 minutes or until the eggs are firm.

1 serving = 1 bite

DOSE: 1 Spinach Artichoke Bite provides about 5 mg THC, if you have used the Recommended Carrier Amounts table (page 9) to make the Canna Ghee.

STORAGE: Transfer the cooled bites to an airtight container. Seal, label, and refrigerate the container, out of the reach of children, for up to 1 week.

TO FREEZE: Wrap cooled bites individually in foil and place them in a resealable bag. Label the bag and keep it in the freezer for up to 3 months.

TO REHEAT: Thaw the bites in the refrigerator overnight and heat them, in the foil, in a preheated 325°F (160°C) oven for 10 minutes or until warmed through.

Smoked Salmon Nori Rolls

Juice of ½ lime

2 ripe avocados, pitted, peeled, and sliced

3 tablespoons Canna Oil (page 15)

1 clove garlic, minced

1 teaspoon wasabi paste, optional

8 sheets (8 x 7 inches) nori

½ English cucumber, cut into ⅛-inch sticks

½ pound smoked salmon fillet, cut into 8 pieces

1 carrot, shredded

---

1 serving = 1 roll

DOSE: 1 Smoked Salmon Nori Roll provides about 6 mg THC, if you have used the Recommended Carrier Amounts table (page 9) to make the Canna Oil.

STORAGE: Smoked Salmon Nori Rolls will keep in the fridge for up to 4 days. Nori Rolls do not freeze well, but you can halve the recipe to make 4 rolls.

---

1. Place the lime juice in the bowl of a food processor. Toss the avocado slices with the lime juice in the bowl. Add the Canna Oil, garlic, and wasabi (if using). Pulse 3 or 4 times or until the mixture is smooth. Set the mixture aside.

2. Place a sheet of nori, shiny-side down, on a clean work surface with a short side closest to you. Spread 2 tablespoons of the avocado mixture on the nori, leaving a clean 1-inch border at the top. Arrange 6 to 8 cucumber sticks on top of the avocado mixture. Layer 1 piece of salmon on top of the cucumber sticks and sprinkle with carrot shreds.

3. Using your fingers, moisten the strip at the top of the nori sheet with water. Roll the nori sheet over the filling, starting from the edge closest to you. Press the moistened strip over the roll to seal it. Place the roll seam-side down and, using a sharp knife, cut the roll in half. Repeat with the remaining nori sheets and filling.

4. Eat the nori rolls immediately or transfer them to an airtight container. Label the container and keep it in the refrigerator, out of the reach of children.

Recipe Note

- Nori sushi sheets are made from kelp, which is a sea vegetable with a salty, nutty flavor. Look for paper-thin nori sheets in specialty or Asian food shops. If you can't find nori, use rice paper wrappers or a leaf from Boston, Bibb, or iceberg lettuce.

>>> Turkey Meatballs

1¼ pounds lean ground turkey

2 tablespoons Canna Oil (page 15)

2 cups shredded cabbage

1 cup shredded carrot

1 small onion, finely chopped

1 clove garlic, minced

½ cup large-flake rolled oats

¼ cup tomato salsa

1 teaspoon sea salt

---

1 serving = 2 meatballs

DOSE: 2 Turkey Meatballs provide about 5 mg THC, if you have used the Recommended Carrier Amounts table (page 9) to make the Canna Oil.

STORAGE: Transfer the cooled meatballs to an airtight container. Label the container and keep it in the refrigerator, out of the reach of children, for up to 4 days.

TO FREEZE: Wrap the meatballs individually in foil and place them in a resealable bag. Label the bag and keep it in the freezer for up to 3 months.

TO REHEAT: Heat the frozen meatballs, in the foil, at 325°F (160°C) for 20 minutes or until warm.

1. Preheat the oven to 350°F (180°C). Lightly oil or line a 12-cup muffin pan with paper liners.

2. Combine the turkey, Canna Oil, cabbage, carrot, onion, and garlic in a large bowl. Sprinkle the oats, salsa, and salt on top and, using your hands or a large spoon, stir the mixture to thoroughly integrate all the ingredients.

3. Spoon the turkey mixture into the prepared muffin pan using a ¼-cup measure. Bake the meatballs in the preheated oven for 30 minutes or until they're firm and the edges are lightly browned. Transfer the meatballs to a wire rack and let them cool for 5 minutes before serving.

Recipe Notes

- Two meatballs are not enough to be considered much more than a tantalizing appetizer. If you want to make a meal of these delicious meatballs, replace the Canna Oil with extra-virgin olive oil.

- To add a serving of Cannabis to non-Cannabis meatballs, serve them with Canna Churri (page 45), Canna Hot Sauce (page 107), or Canna Salsa (page 113).

- If you replace regular salsa with a Canna Salsa, be sure to replace the Canna Oil with non-Cannabis oil, such as extra-virgin olive oil, avocado oil, or coconut oil.

Wild Salmon Cakes

->>>

Makes: 20 cakes

¾ cup plain panko or gluten-free breadcrumbs

⅓ cup Canna Ghee (page 16) or Canna Oil (page 15)

1 egg, lightly beaten

¼ cup chopped fresh parsley

2 tablespoons mayonnaise

2 green onions, finely chopped

1 tablespoon Dijon mustard

1 can (12 ounces) wild salmon, drained (see Recipe Note below)

Olive oil

Recipe Note

- Drain the salmon (reserve the liquid for another use or discard it) and use all the solids in the can.

1. Preheat the oven to 400°F (200°C). Line a rimmed baking sheet with parchment paper. Spread the panko in a shallow pan.

2. Combine the Canna Ghee, egg, parsley, mayonnaise, onions, and mustard in a large bowl. Add the salmon (including the bones if present) and, using a fork, stir well, making sure that the salmon is broken up into small pieces.

3. Measure 1 heaping tablespoon of the salmon mixture and roll it between the palms of your hands to form a ball. Dredge the ball in the panko and press into a 1-inch-thick cake. Place the cake on the prepared baking sheet. Repeat with the remaining mixture until you've used up all of it. Lightly spray or brush the top of the cakes with oil. At this point you can freeze the cakes for use on another day, if desired (see To Freeze below).

4. Bake the cakes in the preheated oven for 12 minutes. Turn over the cakes and bake them for another 5 minutes or until they've turned light golden. Let the cakes cool on a baking sheet for 5 minutes before serving.

1 serving = 2 cakes

DOSE: 2 Wild Salmon Cakes deliver roughly 6 mg THC, if you have used the Recommended Carrier Amounts table (page 9) to make the Canna Ghee.

STORAGE: Transfer the cooled cakes to an airtight container. Seal, label, and refrigerate the container, out of the reach of children, for up to 1 week.

TO FREEZE: Omit step 4 and place the cakes on the baking sheet in the freezer for 15 minutes. Wrap the cakes individually in plastic wrap and then transfer the cakes to a labeled container or a resealable bag. They'll keep in the freezer for up to 3 months.

TO COOK THE FROZEN CAKES: Preheat the oven to 350°F (180°C). Remove the plastic wrap, place the cakes in a heatproof dish, and bake them for 35 minutes or until they're golden and heated through.

>>> # Tomatoes Stuffed with Tuna

Makes: 3 tomatoes

1 cup water

½ cup quinoa, rinsed and drained

½ teaspoon sea salt

3 tomatoes

½ avocado

1 tablespoon freshly squeezed lemon juice

½ red onion, finely chopped

¼ cup mayonnaise

1 tablespoon Canna Oil (page 15)

1 can (5 ounces) tuna, drained

3 tablespoons chopped pistachios

---

1 serving = 1 tomato

DOSE: 1 Tomato Stuffed with Tuna provides about 5 mg THC, if you have used the Recommended Carrier Amounts table (page 9) to make the Canna Oil.

STORAGE: Transfer the stuffed tomatoes to a covered container. Label the container, and keep it in the refrigerator, out of the reach of children, for up to 2 days.

---

1. Combine the water and quinoa in a saucepan. Add the salt and bring the water to a boil over medium-high heat. Cover the pan, reduce the heat to medium-low, and let the liquid simmer for 10 to 15 minutes or until it has been completely absorbed and the quinoa is tender. Remove the pan from the heat and set it aside to cool.

2. Meanwhile, core the tomatoes. Discard the cores and scoop the flesh out of the tomatoes into a medium bowl, leaving the tomatoes whole. Set the tomatoes upright on a plate.

3. Peel, pit, and chop the avocado. Place it in the bowl with the tomato flesh. Add the lemon juice, onion, mayonnaise, and Canna Oil to the bowl and stir well. Add the tuna and flake it, using a fork, while stirring it into the mixture in the bowl. Divide the mixture into 3 even portions and spoon it into the tomatoes. Sprinkle the pistachios on top.

CHAPTER 5

< **DESSERTS** >

Getting baked is all about sweet pleasure in small bites. Indeed, the Cannabis tradition has its past firmly rooted in brownies and other sugary treats. A Google search of "Cannabis Brownies" turned up 1.7 million results, which is why I developed a bit of a twist on the ubiquitous Cannabis brownie. My Brownie TastyBits (page 148) enjoy a hit of canna peanut butter with double chocolate and a bonus: They are conveniently no-bake. If you're a traditionalist, see my notes for making Cannabis brownies using your own favorite recipe or a boxed brownie mix.

Gummies are the number one edible product in all states, according to Green Entrepreneur (see Bibliography, page 209), so try making your own with my adult version (page 150). The Cannabis-infused Salted Caramel Sauce (page 153) may just become your favorite, all-time, over-the-top sweet treat because, apart from being so darned delicious, it is incredibly versatile. Not only can you serve it with the Chocolate Cake (page 151) or add it to smoothies or milk shakes, but you could spoon it over ice cream or any non-Cannabis scone, muffin, tea bread, bar, or cookie. For chocoholics, the Canna Hot Chocolate Sauce (page 155) is divine.

One huge advantage of homemade Cannabis candy/sweet treats is that you get to control the quality and type of strain, as well as the dose. Incredibly, 43 percent of consumers in California's Cannabis edibles market agree that manufacturers need to do a better job of making product dosages reliable and consistent. If you use my Recommended Carrier Amounts table (page 9) and you accurately measure recipe ingredient amounts, you are way ahead of commercial manufacturers! Add to that the fact that you will be using whole flower infusions, and suddenly homemade sweets reign supreme.

< 139 >

Ending a meal on a sweet-high note can be a very pleasant experience. My only advice is that since you can make your own, using any available Cannabis flower and ratio of THC to CBD, keep in mind that an after-lunch sweet or an after-dinner treat might work best if you use a sativa-dominant strain. Save your indica-dominant Canna Butter for making before-bed treats. Indulge!

⇢>>> Almond Refrigerator Cookies

¼ cup softened Canna Coco Oil (page 13)

1 egg

1 tablespoon molasses

½ cup coconut or granulated sugar

1 cup all-purpose flour or gluten-free flour blend

½ teaspoon baking soda

½ teaspoon sea salt

¼ teaspoon ground nutmeg

⅓ cup coarsely chopped almonds

---

1 serving = 2 or 3 cookies

DOSE: 2 Almond Refrigerator Cookies provide about 4 mg THC, and 3 cookies will deliver 6 mg THC if you have used the Recommended Carrier Amounts table (page 9) to make the Canna Coco Oil.

STORAGE: Refrigerate the wrapped dough and use within 2 weeks. Keep baked cookies in an airtight container at room temperature for 1 week or in the refrigerator, out of the reach of children, for up to 2 weeks. Frozen dough will keep in the freezer for up to 3 months.

---

1. Beat the Canna Coco Oil and egg together in a large bowl, using a wooden spoon. Stir in the molasses and sugar and beat until creamy.

2. Whisk together the flour, baking soda, salt, and nutmeg in a separate bowl. Sprinkle the flour mixture over the creamed Canna Coco Oil mixture and stir well. Stir in the almonds.

3. Scrape the dough into the center of a piece of waxed paper, using a rubber spatula. Seal and refrigerate for 30 minutes. Cut the dough into 2 even pieces. Place each piece on a square of waxed paper and roll it into a cylinder 1½ inches in diameter. Wrap, label, and refrigerate 1 roll out of the reach of children for up to 2 weeks.

4. Cut the remaining roll into ⅛-inch slices, wrap it in waxed paper, label it, and place in a resealable bag. Freeze it for up to 3 months. When you're ready to use it, thaw it in the refrigerator and bake it according to step 5.

5. Preheat the oven to 375°F (190°C). Slice the refrigerated roll into ⅛-inch slices and arrange some or all of them on a parchment-lined baking sheet. Bake for 8 minutes or until they're lightly browned. Let them cool on the baking sheet for 5 minutes and transfer to a wire rack to cool completely.

>>>> # Apricot-Almond Chews

1½ cups granola, homemade or store-bought (see Recipe Note below)

¼ cup chopped almonds

¼ cup chopped mixed dried fruit

2 tablespoons ground flaxseed

¼ cup Canna Honey (page 24) or Canna Ghee (page 16)

1 teaspoon pure vanilla extract

---

1 serving = 2 chews

DOSE: 2 Apricot-Almond Chews provide about 5 mg THC if you have used the Recommended Carrier Amounts table (page 9) to make the Canna Honey.

STORAGE: Keep the chews in an airtight container in the refrigerator, out of the reach of children, for 14 days, or freeze for up to 3 months.

---

1. Line a rimmed baking sheet with parchment paper.

2. Combine granola, almonds, dried fruit, and flaxseed in a food processor and pulse 2 or 3 times or until mixed. Drizzle the Canna Honey and vanilla on top, and pulse 2 or 3 times to mix.

3. Measure 2 tablespoons of dough and roll it between the palms of your hands. Place the ball on the prepared baking sheet. Flatten using the oiled tines of a fork. Repeat until the remaining dough is used up. Refrigerate for at least 1 hour before serving.

Recipe Note

- Use plain granola or a mixture that contains lots of nuts and fruit. You can also substitute an equal amount of rice cereal for the granola in this recipe.

>>> Baked Custard

1 tablespoon extra-virgin coconut oil or olive oil, for greasing cups

1½ cups milk

2 tablespoons Canna Ghee (page 16) or Canna Oil (page 15)

3 eggs

⅓ cup coconut or granulated sugar

½ teaspoon pure vanilla extract

Pinch of salt

---

1 serving = 1 custard

DOSE: 1 Baked Custard provides about 6 mg THC if you have used the Recommended Carrier Amounts table (page 9) to make the Canna Ghee.

STORAGE: Transfer custards to an airtight container, label, and keep in the refrigerator, out of the reach of children, for up to 5 days. Custards do not freeze well.

---

1. Preheat the oven to 350°F (180°C). Lightly grease 4 custard cups or ramekins. Arrange them in a 3-inch deep baking pan so that they are not touching each other or the sides of the pan. Bring a full kettle of water to a boil.

2. Combine the milk and Canna Ghee in a saucepan. Heat over medium-high heat, stirring frequently, for 6 minutes or until the milk is steaming, not bubbling. Remove from the heat.

3. Combine the eggs, sugar, vanilla, and salt in a large bowl and beat with a fork until blended, not foamy. Gradually stir in the hot milk until the sugar is dissolved. Divide the mixture evenly among the 4 custard cups.

4. Place the baking pan with the custard cups in the center of the preheated oven. Pour the boiled water into the baking pan until it reaches within ½ inch of the tops of the cups. Bake for 25 minutes or until a knife inserted in the center of a custard comes out clean. Centers will be soft. Remove the baking pan from the oven and transfer the cups to a wire rack to cool. Serve warm or refrigerate until chilled.

Banana Cherry Cookies

Makes: 12 cookies

3 ripe bananas

¼ cup Canna Ghee (page 16)
or Canna Coco Oil (page 13)

¼ cup almond milk

1 teaspoon pure almond or
vanilla extract

2 cups large-flake rolled oats

½ teaspoon baking soda

½ teaspoon sea salt

½ cup dried chopped dried
cherries or cranberries

---

1 serving = 1 cookie

DOSE: 1 Banana Cherry
Cookie provides about
5 mg THC if you have used
the Recommended Carrier
Amounts table (page 9) to
make the Canna Ghee.

STORAGE: Transfer cooled
cookies to an airtight
container, label, and keep
at room temperature, out of
the reach of children, for up
to 10 days.

TO FREEZE: Freeze cookies
on a rimmed baking sheet
for 30 minutes. Transfer to
a resealable bag, seal, label,
and keep frozen for up to
3 months.

1. Preheat the oven to 350°F (180°C). Line 2 baking sheets with parchment paper.

2. Blend the bananas in a food processor. Add the Canna Ghee, milk, and almond extract and process for 30 seconds or until well blended. Add the oats, baking soda, and salt and pulse 3 or 4 times or until well blended.

3. Scrape the mixture into a bowl using a rubber spatula. Stir in the cherries. Scoop 2 tablespoons of the dough using a 1-ounce ice-cream scoop or tablespoons and roll it into a ball. Drop each ball onto the prepared baking sheets, spacing them about 2 inches apart. Lightly flatten each ball of dough with the oiled tines of a fork.

4. Bake 1 sheet at a time in the preheated oven for 20 minutes or until the cookies are lightly browned. Let them cool on the baking sheet for 3 minutes before transferring to a wire rack to cool completely.

>>> Canna Banana Bites

¼ cup Canna Ghee (page 16) or Canna Coco Oil (page 13)

2 tablespoons mashed ripe banana

2 tablespoons pineapple or orange juice

1 tablespoon almond milk

1 egg

1 cup all-purpose flour or gluten-free flour blend

¼ teaspoon baking soda

1 cup shredded unsweetened coconut

---

1 serving = 1 bite

DOSE: 1 Canna Banana Bite provides about 6 mg THC if you have used the Recommended Carrier Amounts table (page 9) to make the Canna Ghee.

STORAGE: Transfer to an airtight container, label, and refrigerate for up to 2 weeks, out of the reach of children.

TO FREEZE: Arrange bites in a single layer on a rimmed baking sheet and freeze for 30 minutes. Transfer to a resealable bag, label, and freeze for up to 5 months.

1. Preheat the oven to 350°F (180°C). Line a baking sheet with parchment paper.

2. Combine the Canna Ghee and banana in a food processor and pulse 2 or 3 times to mix. Add the juice, milk, and egg and pulse 1 or 2 times to mix. Sift the flour and baking soda over the mixture in the food processor. Pulse for 20 seconds or until well blended. Scrape the mixture into a bowl. Stir in the coconut.

3. Scoop up 2 tablespoons of the mixture. Scrape the packed mixture out of the tablespoon, roll into a ball between the palms of your hands, and drop onto the prepared baking sheet. Repeat until the entire mixture has been used up.

4. Bake in preheated oven for 10 minutes or until lightly golden around the edges.

Recipe Note

- You may find it hard to eat only 1 bite at a serving (they're that good), so consider making 1 batch or half the recipe using Canna Ghee and another batch or half a batch using regular, non-Cannabis butter.

>>>> Brownie TastyBits

1 square (1 ounce) semisweet baking chocolate

½ cup peanut or cashew butter

¼ cup Canna Coco Oil (page 13) or Canna Ghee (page 16)

¼ cup confectioners' sugar

1 teaspoon pure vanilla extract

1½ cups large-flake rolled oats

3 tablespoons dark cocoa powder

1 teaspoon instant espresso powder, optional (see Recipe Note opposite)

½ teaspoon sea salt

1 to 2 tablespoons organic coconut flour

About ½ cup sunflower seeds or finely chopped cashews or peanuts, for dusting, optional

1. Melt the chocolate in the top of a double boiler, over boiling water. Remove from the heat and set aside to cool to lukewarm.

2. Combine the peanut butter, Canna Coco Oil, sugar, and vanilla in a food processor. Drizzle the melted chocolate over the peanut butter mixture and pulse for 30 seconds or until well combined. Add the oats, cocoa, instant espresso (if using), and salt. Pulse for 30 seconds or until well mixed.

3. *Test the consistency:* If it's too wet, add coconut flour, 1 tablespoon at a time, but the mixture needs to hold together, so be careful not to add too much flour or the dough will be dry and crumbly. Scoop out 2 tablespoons of dough and roll it into a ball between the palms of your hands. If desired, place seeds or chopped nuts into a shallow bowl and roll each ball around in the nuts to coat them.

— *To make Cannabis-infused brownies using your own favorite recipe:* Use ¼ cup Canna Coco Oil or Canna Ghee in your recipe, and if your recipe calls for more than ¼ cup butter (or another fat), use ¼ cup Canna fat and make up the difference with non-infused fat. If you use ¼ cup Canna fat, to make each serving equal 5 mg THC, your recipe must make 12 servings. So if you have used ¼ cup Canna Butter in your favorite recipe, make sure to divide the brownies into 12 equal servings.

— *To make Cannabis-infused brownies from a boxed brownie mix:* Melt ¼ cup Canna Ghee and ¼ cup non-Cannabis butter in a saucepan over low heat and set aside to cool. Mix 2 cups of the boxed brownie mix with the melted butter in a medium bowl. Beat in 2 eggs, one at a time, 1 teaspoon pure vanilla extract, and 1 tablespoon water. You can add ½ cup chocolate chips or

148 < COOKING WITH CANNABIS

1 serving = 1 TastyBit

DOSE: 1 Brownie TastyBit provides about 5 mg THC if you have used the Recommended Carrier Amounts table (page 9) to make the Canna Coco Oil.

Recipe Note

- Instant espresso powder is available in most supermarkets or online or you can use finely ground espresso from a coffeemaker pod. I use it here to darken the color of the brownie bits, bring out the chocolate taste, and, at the same time, help mask the flavor of the Cannabis.

½ cup chopped nuts, if desired. Spread in a lightly oiled 8 x 8-inch baking pan and bake at 350°F (180°C) for about 40 minutes. Set aside to cool. Cut into sixteen 2-inch squares. Each 2-inch square will deliver about 4 mg THC if you have used the Recommended Carrier Amounts table (page 9) to make the Canna Ghee.

>>>> Cannabis Gummies

Olive oil

1 envelope (3 ounces)
flavored jelly powder (see
Recipe Notes below)

1 envelope (¼-ounce)
unflavored gelatin

⅓ cup pineapple, orange,
grape, or cherry juice,
chilled (see Recipe Notes
below)

¼ teaspoon freshly squeezed
lemon juice, optional (see
Recipe Notes below)

2 tablespoons Canna Tincture
(pages 33–34; see Recipe
Notes below)

About ¼ cup cornstarch for
dusting, optional

---

1 serving = 1 gummie

DOSE: 1 Cannabis Gummie
provides roughly 5 mg
THC if you have used the
Recommended Carrier
Amounts table (page 9) to
make the Canna Tincture.

STORAGE: Gummies will
keep in the refrigerator for
up to 3 weeks. Cannabis
Gummies will harden in the
refrigerator the longer they
are stored. Label and keep
out of the reach of children.

---

1. Soak the corner of a paper towel with olive oil and lightly oil a
   6-inch square baking pan.

2. Whisk together the jelly powder, gelatin, and cold juice in a bowl.
   Set aside for 10 minutes to soften the gelatin.

3. Gently heat the bowl over a pan of simmering water for 2 minutes,
   or microwave for 30 seconds on full power. Remove the bowl from
   the heat and stir the mixture. Repeat the heating process until the
   gelatin granules are melted and the mixture is clear. Stir in the
   lemon juice (if using) and the Canna Tincture.

4. Pour the mixture into the prepared pan and refrigerate for 2 to
   3 hours or overnight. Using a ruler, cut jelly into six 2 x 3-inch
   squares. Add the cornstarch (if using) to a small, shallow bowl and
   dust the gummies in the cornstarch.

5. Transfer the gummies to an airtight container, label, and
   refrigerate, out of the reach of children.

Recipe Notes

- To make these gummies, you will need a 6-inch square baking pan.
  If you use a larger pan, the gummies will be thinner in depth and
  larger.

- Do not substitute Canna Coco Oil or Canna Ghee for the Canna
  Tincture in this recipe.

- Use any color of flavored jelly powder. For light colors, use orange
  or apple juice; for dark colors, use cherry or grape juice.

- For sour-tasting jellies, add ¼ teaspoon or more of freshly
  squeezed lemon juice.

Chocolate Cake with Salted Caramel Sauce

Makes: 1 cake, no THC

6 tablespoons unsalted
butter, plus more for
greasing the pan(s)

⅓ cup dark cocoa powder,
plus extra for dusting
the pan(s)

3 squares (1 ounce each)
bittersweet baking
chocolate

⅔ cup water

1 cup granulated sugar

⅓ cup extra-virgin olive oil or
hemp oil

1¼ cups all-purpose flour

2 teaspoons baking powder

1 teaspoon sea salt

2 eggs

⅓ cup plain yogurt or
buttermilk (see Recipe
Notes on page 152)

1 batch Salted Caramel
Sauce (recipe follows) or
Canna Hot Chocolate Sauce
(page 155)

1 batch Chocolate Filling
(page 154) or 1 cup jam
(for a 2-layer cake; see
Recipe Notes on page 152)

STORAGE: Store leftover
cake in an airtight container
for up to 5 days.

1. Preheat the oven to 300°F (150°C). Lightly butter a 9-inch round cake pan or two 8-inch round cake pans and line the bottom(s) with parchment paper. Butter the paper and dust with cocoa powder. (Note that if you use 2 layer cake pans, you will need to make a Chocolate Filling (page 153), per step 5, or use jam between the layers.)

2. Combine bittersweet chocolate and butter in a large saucepan and melt over medium-low heat. Remove from the heat, add the water, and stir until smooth. Whisk in the sugar and oil and set aside to cool completely.

3. Meanwhile, combine the flour, baking powder, ⅓ cocoa, and salt in a small bowl.

4. Whisk the eggs into the cooled chocolate mixture, one at a time. Sprinkle the flour mixture onto the chocolate mixture and gently stir to mix. Stir in the yogurt.

5. Scrape the batter into prepared pan(s) and bake on the middle shelf of the preheated oven for 40 to 45 minutes or until a toothpick comes out clean. Cool on a rack for 10 minutes and then turn it out onto a serving plate to cool completely. Meanwhile, if you baked 2 layers, use the Chocolate Filling and follow directions for assembling cake layers on page 154.

6. Slice and serve with Salted Caramel Sauce.

(recipe continued on following page)

Recipe Notes

- This makes a dense cake, even if you choose to use buttermilk instead of yogurt. Buttermilk is thick, fermented dairy milk. If you do not have buttermilk, stir 1 teaspoon freshly squeezed lemon juice or apple cider vinegar into ⅓ cup regular milk.

- If you have a deep 9-inch round pan, this recipe makes one cake that needs no icing, due to the richness of the Salted Caramel Sauce.

- Do not try to bake this in 1 standard 8-inch layer cake pan. Instead, use two 8-inch cake pans and make the Chocolate Filling (page 154) or use strawberry or raspberry jam to spread between the layers.

SALTED CARAMEL SAUCE

¼ cup water

1 cup granulated sugar

⅔ cup whipping cream (36% butterfat)

2 tablespoons unsalted butter

2 tablespoons Canna Ghee (page 16)

1 teaspoon pure vanilla extract

1 to 1½ teaspoons kosher salt or coarse sea salt, or to taste

---

1 serving = ¼ cup

DOSE: ¼ cup Salted Caramel Sauce provides roughly 5 mg THC if you have used the Recommended Carrier Amounts table (page 9) to make the Canna Ghee.

---

1. Bring the water to a simmer in a 5-cup saucepan set over medium-high heat. Stir in the sugar and bring to a boil, stirring constantly. Once at a boil, stop stirring and let the sugar-water mixture cook for about 6 minutes, turning the heat down if the boil is furiously rapid.

2. Watch closely and when the mixture turns color slightly, remove the pan from the heat and swirl it to evenly distribute the light amber areas. Return to the heat and watch closely for 30 seconds to 1 minute until the mixture turns a medium amber color, then immediately remove from the heat.

3. Slowly whisk in the cream, a small amount at a time, whisking constantly because the sugar mixture will foam up. One at a time, whisk in the butter, Canna Ghee, vanilla, and 1 teaspoon salt. Cool slightly and taste. Add more salt, if desired.

Recipe Notes

- Use a 5-cup or larger saucepan to allow for the foaming that takes place when you add the whipping cream.

- I cook with gas, which is very responsive, so in step 1, if using an electric burner, you may need to cook the sugar water for longer than 6 minutes before you start to see any coloring. But be aware that once the mixture starts to color, it changes quickly and turns brown (which you don't want) fast.

>>> Chocolate Filling

Makes: 1 cup

⅓ cup granulated sugar

1 tablespoon cornstarch

Pinch of salt

¾ cup milk

1 egg yolk

1 square (1 ounce) semisweet baking chocolate, coarsely chopped

1 teaspoon pure vanilla extract

1. Combine the sugar, cornstarch, and salt in a saucepan. In a small bowl, whisk together the milk and the egg yolk. Slowly whisk the milk mixture into the sugar mixture. Add the chocolate and cook over medium heat, stirring constantly until the mixture boils. Boil, stirring constantly for 1 minute or until the chocolate flecks disappear.

2. Remove from the heat and stir in the vanilla. Pour into a bowl and press plastic wrap directly onto the surface of the filling to prevent a skin from forming as the filling cools. When the filling is cool, chill it for at least an hour or up to overnight in the refrigerator.

3. *To assemble a layer cake:* Place 1 cake layer, rounded side up, on a serving plate. Spread the chilled filling on top of the cake layer, using all the filling and spreading the filling right to the edges. Place the second cake layer directly on top of the filling, rounded side down (both of the rounded sides are held together with filling). Keep the cake chilled until it's ready to serve with Salted Caramel Sauce (page 153) or Canna Hot Chocolate Sauce (opposite).

>>>> Canna Hot Chocolate Sauce

Makes: 2 cups

⅔ cup granulated sugar

2 tablespoons cornstarch

½ cup unsweetened
cocoa powder

1½ cups almond milk
(see Recipe Notes below)

12 caramel squares,
unwrapped

2 tablespoons Canna Ghee
(page 16; see Recipe Notes
below)

½ teaspoon sea salt,
or to taste

1 serving = ⅓ cup

DOSE: ⅓ cup Canna
Hot Chocolate Sauce
provides roughly 5 mg
THC if you have used the
Recommended Carrier
Amounts table (page 9) to
make the Canna Ghee.

1. Combine the sugar, cornstarch, and cocoa in a bowl and whisk until blended. Set aside.

2. Heat the milk in a saucepan over medium heat. Add the caramel squares to the milk as it heats. Cook, whisking constantly for about 5 minutes or until the caramel squares have completely melted. Turn the heat to medium-low. Whisk in the dry ingredients and cook, stirring constantly for 4 minutes or until the mixture has thickened. Add the Canna Ghee and whisk for a minute or until the mixture is glossy. Taste and add salt as desired.

3. Pour into a heatproof jar or small jug and serve immediately.

Recipe Notes

- This sauce is best served hot. Drizzle it over ice cream or stir it into hot milk or cocoa. Serve it warm over bars or Chocolate Cake (page 151), or mix into milk shakes or cold milk.

- With the caramel, the flavor is buttery and rich, but not screaming chocolate. If you want a more intense chocolate experience, melt 1 square (1 ounce) unsweetened baking chocolate with the caramel squares in step 2.

- You can use Canna Coco Oil (page 13) if you want a vegan sauce, but I prefer the extra hit of nutty butter from Canna Ghee.

Chocolate Yogurt Cup with Fruit and Nuts

Makes: 1 cup

1 cup vanilla or plain
Greek-style yogurt

1 tablespoon Power Herb
Cocoa Blend (page 174)
or cocoa powder

1 tablespoon pure maple
syrup

1 teaspoon Canna Oil
(page 15)

¼ cup chopped fresh fruit
(apples, oranges, berries,
banana, kiwi, peaches, etc.)

½ cup coarsely chopped
almonds

1 serving = 1 cup

DOSE: 1 Chocolate Yogurt
Cup provides about 5 mg
THC if you have used the
Recommended Carrier
Amounts table (page 9) to
make Canna Oil.

— Combine yogurt, Power Herb Cocoa Blend, maple syrup, and Canna Oil in a dessert bowl or a 2-cup Mason jar. Stir well. Top with fruit and nuts.

>>>> Coconut Bars

Makes: 12 bars

¼ cup Canna Ghee (page 16)
or Canna Coco Oil (page 13)

¼ cup unsalted butter

1 cup graham cracker
crumbs (from about
8 whole graham crackers)

1 cup flaked, sweetened
coconut

1 cup white chocolate chips,
optional

1 cup toffee pieces or
butterscotch chips

1 cup chopped pecans or
walnuts

1 can (14 ounces) sweetened
condensed milk

1 serving = 1 bar

DOSE: 1 Coconut Bar
provides about 5 mg
THC if you have used the
Recommended Carrier
Amounts table (page 9) to
make Canna Ghee.

STORAGE: Bars will keep in
an airtight container for up
to 5 days and up to 10 days
if refrigerated.

1. Preheat the oven to 350°F (180°C).

2. Combine the Canna Ghee and butter in a heatproof 12 x 9-inch
baking pan and heat over medium-low heat until the butter is
melted. Remove from the heat and sprinkle the graham cracker
crumbs on top, mixing well using a fork. Press the crumb mixture
evenly over the bottom of the pan.

3. Evenly sprinkle the coconut over the graham cracker base. Evenly
sprinkle the chocolate chips (if using) over the coconut . Evenly
sprinkle the toffee over chocolate chips. Evenly sprinkle the
pecans over the toffee. Drizzle the condensed milk evenly over the
entire pan.

4. Bake in the preheated oven for 25 minutes. Cool in the pan and cut
into 3-inch squares (use a ruler).

>>>> French Vanilla Ice Cream

2 cups whole milk

1¾ cups heavy whipping cream (36% butterfat)

¼ cup Canna Cream (page 21)

1 vanilla bean, split in half

13 egg yolks

1 cup granulated sugar

½ cup liquid honey

½ teaspoon pure vanilla extract

½ teaspoon sea salt

---

1 serving = ½ cup

DOSE: ½ cup French Vanilla Ice Cream provides 6 mg THC if you have used the Recommended Carrier Amounts table (page 9) to make the Canna Cream.

---

1. Combine the milk, whipping cream, Canna Cream, and vanilla bean in a large saucepan. Warm over low heat for 35 to 40 minutes. Check occasionally and do not let the mixture scald or boil. Remove the bean halves and scrape the seeds back into the cream mixture.

2. Meanwhile, lightly beat the egg yolks in a large bowl. Whisk in the sugar until blended.

3. Bring the cream mixture to a boil, remove from the heat, and slowly pour it into the yolk mixture, whisking constantly until completely combined. Pour the mixture back into the saucepan and cook over medium heat, stirring constantly for 25 minutes or until thickened.

4. Remove from the heat and stir in the honey, vanilla extract, and salt. Set aside to cool. Cover and refrigerate for 60 minutes or until cold.

5. Transfer to an ice-cream maker and freeze according to manufacturer's instructions. Use immediately or transfer to an airtight container and freeze for up to 1 month. Soften at room temperature for about 20 minutes before serving.

>>>> Gingerbread Squares

1 cup unsalted butter,
at room temperature

½ cup **Canna Ghee** (page 16)
or **Canna Coco Oil** (page 13)

¼ cup coconut or brown
sugar

¼ cup applesauce

¼ cup molasses

1 large egg

1 teaspoon pure almond
extract

2 tablespoons grated fresh
ginger or 2 teaspoons
ground ginger

1½ cups all-purpose flour

½ teaspoon ground cinnamon

¼ teaspoon ground cloves

¼ teaspoon baking powder

¼ teaspoon baking soda

½ teaspoon sea salt

Pinch of black pepper

1. Preheat the oven to 350°F (180°C). Grease a large baking pan (see Recipe Note below).

2. Combine the butter, Canna Ghee, sugar, applesauce, molasses, egg, almond extract, and ginger in a food processor and process until smooth. Set aside, keeping the mixture in the food processor bowl.

3. Combine the flour, cinnamon, cloves, baking powder, baking soda, salt, and pepper in a bowl. Spoon over the butter mixture in the food processor and pulse 3 or 4 times or until well combined.

4. Scrape the batter into the prepared pan using a rubber spatula and bake in the preheated oven for 10 minutes or until lightly browned. Set aside to cool for 5 minutes. Cut into eighteen 2- x 3-inch squares (use a ruler). Transfer the squares to a wire rack to cool completely.

---

1 serving = 1 square

DOSE: 1 Gingerbread Square provides about 6 mg THC if you have used the Recommended Carrier Amounts table (page 9) to make the Canna Ghee.

STORAGE: Transfer the cooled squares to an airtight container, label, and refrigerate, out of the reach of children, for up to 4 days.

TO FREEZE: Arrange squares in a single layer on a parchment-lined, rimmed baking sheet and freeze for 30 minutes. Transfer to a resealable bag, seal, label, and freeze for up to 3 months.

TO REHEAT: Preheat the oven to 350°F (180°C). Place frozen square(s) on a baking sheet and bake for 7 to 12 minutes or until heated through.

Recipe Note

- I suggest that you use a 9 x 12-inch or a 9 x 13-inch baking pan to bake these squares. If you use a smaller pan, you may need to bake them for a longer time (about 12 minutes). Just be sure to cut into 18 squares (use a ruler) so that the dose is correct per square.

>>>> Raisin-Oatmeal Cookies

Makes: 12 cookies

2 tablespoons ground
flaxseeds

½ cup plain or vanilla
nondairy milk, divided

1 cup large-flake rolled oats

¾ cup all-purpose flour or
gluten-free flour blend

½ teaspoon baking powder

½ teaspoon baking soda

¼ teaspoon ground allspice

¼ teaspoon ground cinnamon

¼ teaspoon sea salt

½ cup golden raisins

¼ cup Canna Ghee (page 16)
or Canna Coco Oil, softened
(page 13)

¼ cup softened extra-virgin
coconut oil

⅔ cup coconut or
brown sugar

½ teaspoon pure
vanilla extract

1. Preheat the oven to 400°F (200°C). Lightly oil 2 baking sheets.

2. Combine the flaxseeds and 3 tablespoons of milk in a small bowl.
   Set aside for 10 minutes or until thick and gel-like.

3. Whisk together the rolled oats, flour, baking powder, baking soda,
   allspice, cinnamon, and salt in another bowl. Stir in the raisins and
   set aside.

4. Combine the Canna Chee, coconut oil, sugar, and vanilla in a large
   bowl and beat together using a wooden spoon until blended. Beat
   in the flaxseed mixture. Sprinkle half the flour mixture on top
   and beat well. Add the remaining milk and beat well. Sprinkle the
   remaining flour mixture on top and beat well.

5. Scoop up 2 tablespoons of dough, roll it into a ball, and drop it
   onto the prepared baking sheet (a 1-ounce ice-cream scoop works
   well), spacing the cookies 2 inches apart. Press the cookies using
   the oiled tines of a fork to between ¼ inch and ½ inch thick.

6. Bake 1 sheet at a time in the center of the preheated oven for
   8 minutes or until lightly browned. Remove from the oven and let
   the cookies cool on the pan for 7 minutes or until firm enough to
   transfer to a wire rack to cool completely.

1 serving = 1 cookie

DOSE: 1 Raisin Oatmeal Cookie provides about 5 mg THC if you have used the
Recommended Carrier Amounts table (page 9) to make the Canna Ghee.

STORAGE: Transfer the cookies to an airtight container, label, and refrigerate
for up to 1 week, out of the reach of children.

TO FREEZE: Arrange the baked cookies in a single layer on a rimmed baking
sheet and freeze for 30 minutes. Transfer to a resealable bag, label, and freeze
for up to 4 months.

Shortbread Cookies

Makes: 24 cookies

¼ cup Canna Ghee
(page 16)

½ cup unsalted butter,
softened

½ cup confectioners' sugar
or fine granulated sugar

2½ cups rice flour
(see Recipe Note below)

½ teaspoon sea salt

---

1 serving = 2 cookies

DOSE: 2 Shortbread
Cookies provide about
5 mg THC if you have used
the Recommended Carrier
Amounts table (page 9) to
make the Canna Ghee.

STORAGE: Transfer the
cooled cookies to an
airtight container, label,
and refrigerate, out of the
reach of children, for up to
2 weeks.

TO FREEZE: Arrange the
cooled cookies on a rimmed
baking sheet and freeze for
30 minutes. Transfer to a
resealable bag, seal, label,
and freeze for up to
4 months.

---

1. Preheat the oven to 300°F (150°C). Line a baking sheet with parchment paper. Set aside.

2. Combine the Canna Ghee and butter in a food processor. Add the sugar and process for 30 seconds or until the butter is light and fluffy.

3. Sprinkle the flour and salt over the butter. Pulse 2 or 3 times or until the dry ingredients are well blended.

4. Measure 1 tablespoon of dough and roll it between the palms of your hands. Place the ball on the prepared baking sheet. Repeat until all the dough is used up, spacing the balls about 1 inch apart. Lightly press down on each ball with your index finger to make a round cookie, about 1 inch in diameter.

5. Bake in the preheated oven for about 15 minutes, or until firm to the touch (shortbread should be pale in color).

Recipe Note

- Rice flour is an excellent gluten-free option for shortbread and it increases the crunch. You can use cake or pastry flour in this recipe instead of the rice flour.

Makes: 4 halves

Filling

2 tablespoons Canna Ghee
(page 16) or Canna Oil
(page 15)

2 tablespoons chopped
onions

⅓ cup large-flake rolled oats

⅓ cup chopped walnuts

1 tablespoon freshly
squeezed lemon juice

1 teaspoon finely chopped,
candied ginger

½ teaspoon ground cinnamon

Pears

2 pears, halved lengthwise
and cored (see Recipe Note
opposite)

1 tablespoon freshly
squeezed lemon juice

Garnish

¼ cup liquid honey, optional

¼ cup shredded
Cheddar cheese

1. *To make the filling:* Combine the Canna Ghee, onion, oats, walnuts, lemon juice, ginger, and cinnamon in a food processor. Pulse 2 or 3 times, just until uniformly chopped and mixed together. You can make the filling, cover it, and refrigerate it up to 1 day ahead.

2. *To prepare the pears:* Preheat the oven to 400°F (200°C). Line a baking sheet with parchment paper. Using a spoon, scoop out some of the pear flesh to make a cavity for the filling. Set the pear flesh aside to add to the filling in step 3. Arrange the pear halves, cut-side up, on the prepared baking sheet and brush each with lemon juice. Cover the pan with foil and bake in the preheated oven for 15 to 20 minutes or until the pears are tender but offer some resistance when pierced with a sharp knife.

3. Chop the reserved pear flesh, add to the filling, and stir well. Divide the filling into 4 equal portions and spoon each into the pear cavities, mounding it up. Drizzle 1 tablespoon of honey (if using) over each pear and sprinkle each with 1 tablespoon cheese. Reduce the oven temperature to 350°F (180°C) and bake, uncovered, for 5 to 12 minutes or until the filling is bubbling. Remove from the oven and let the pears cool slightly before serving.

1 serving = 1 half

DOSE: Half a Savory Pear provides about 5 mg THC if you have used the Recommended Carrier Amounts table (page 9) to make the Canna Oil.

STORAGE: Keep the pears in an airtight container in the refrigerator, out of the reach of children, for up to 4 days.

TO REHEAT: Place the pear halves in a heatproof dish, cover with foil and bake in a 300°F (150°F) oven for 7 to 12 minutes or until reheated. Or reheat in the microwave in a heatproof dish (no foil) on medium for 4 minutes.

- A sweet, crisp pear such as Bartlett, Bosc, or Green or Red Anjou that is not quite ripe works best in this recipe.

CHAPTER 6

< **Drinks** >

In the commercial arena, Cannabis-infused drinks are and will continue to be big news as more companies gear up to cash in on an ever-expanding market. But, as I see it, crafting a beverage to suit first-time Cannabis adventurers and, at the same time, aiming to satisfy serious, high-tolerance Cannabis pros is impossible. Don't forget, too, that the absentminded ease of sipping something really, really tasty almost guarantees that you'll overindulge—take too much, too quickly—and it all could peak at once . . . two hours later.

Which is why this chapter offers a brilliant solution: You can create a drink that is perfect for the event, just right for your tolerance level, and, most importantly, you can have seconds or thirds that are Cannabis-free.

This chapter is all about enjoyment and wellness in a glass or a cup. It boasts remarkable bedtime teas, warm and chilled infusions, lattes, and cocoa; midday smoothies; and relaxing Cannabis mocktails that deliver exactly the amount of THC with which you are comfortable. In addition, I've added a couple of raw Cannabis juices that take advantage of the healing benefits of THCA.

One of the key factors in creating single-serving, Cannabis-infused drinks is having an oil, honey, whipped cream, simple syrup, or tincture in your pantry. So you might want to brush up on the Cannabis infusions found in chapter 1. If I had to choose only one infusion to use in drinks, it would be the Canna Honey (page 24).

CAUTION: *Never mix Cannabis with alcohol. Apart from the fact that the experiences are not interchangeable, the Cannabis high is not enhanced by alcohol; in fact, I'd say alcohol works against the reflective, healing state induced by Cannabis. Adding an alcohol-based Cannabis tincture is safe because you are only using a very small amount (1 teaspoon or 1 tablespoon at most) of Cannabis-infused alcohol.*

< 165 >

Teas to Ease Into Sleep

->>> Calming Latte

Makes: 1 latte

1 cup almond milk or regular dairy milk

1 teaspoon Canna Honey (page 24)

1 teaspoon powdered ashwagandha, optional (see Recipe Note)

½ teaspoon ground passionflower or valerian, optional (see Recipe Note)

¼ teaspoon ground cardamom

¼ ground cinnamon

⅛ teaspoon ground ginger

---

1 serving = 1 latte

DOSE: 1 Calming Latte provides about 5 mg THC if you have used the Recommended Carrier Amounts table (page 9) to make the Canna Honey.

---

1. Whisk together the milk, Canna Honey, ashwagandha (if using), passionflower (if using), cardamom, cinnamon, and ginger in a saucepan. Heat over medium-high heat, stirring frequently, for 5 minutes or until bubbles form around the inside of the pan.

2. Strain into a cup using a fine-mesh strainer.

Recipe Note

- Ashwagandha, valerian, and passionflower are powerful herbs that herbalists use to treat insomnia. Calming Latte (and all the teas that follow) is a great sleep-inducing drink even without these herbs, especially if you use an indica-dominant Cannabis strain to make the Canna Honey. So try this drink even if you don't have either herb. If you would like to try just one herb, ashwagandha is the most versatile of the two herbs (see Resources, page 210, to purchase it online).

>>>> Cannabis Fruit Juice

(a raw Cannabis recipe)

Makes: 1 large or 2 small glasses, no THC

2 oranges, peeled

1 grapefruit, peeled

1 apple, cored

1 kiwi, peeled

2 or 3 (3-inch-long) fresh
Cannabis roots (see
Recipe Notes)

1. Process the oranges, grapefruit, apple, kiwi, and Cannabis roots using a juicing machine.

2. Whisk and pour into 1 large or 2 smaller glasses.

Recipe Notes

- If you have fresh Cannabis roots, scrub and add them to the juicer. Try using a couple of roots first, then taste and gauge if you like the flavor or want to add more.

- You can roast and dry Cannabis roots (see Pat's Root Beverage Blend, page 173, for how to roast and dry roots) and then powder them. Add about 1 tablespoon powdered Cannabis roots to tea, juice, or smoothies.

Cannabis Vegetable Juice

(a raw Cannabis recipe)

Makes: 1 large or 2 small glasses, no THC

2 stalks kale or Swiss chard

2 carrots

1 beet

1 apple, cored

2 or 3 (3-inch-long) fresh Cannabis roots (see Recipe Notes page 168)

1. Process the kale, carrots, beet, apple, and Cannabis roots using a juicing machine.

2. Whisk and pour into 1 large or 2 smaller glasses.

Golden Latte

Makes: 2 lattes

2 cups regular or vanilla coconut milk or almond milk

1 tablespoon grated fresh turmeric or 1 teaspoon ground turmeric

1 teaspoon grated fresh ginger or ½ teaspoon ground ginger

2 teaspoons Canna Healing Honey (page 25) or Canna Tincture (pages 33–34)

½ teaspoon ground cinnamon

Pinch of ground cloves

Pinch of ground black pepper

1. Combine the milk, turmeric, ginger, Canna Healing Honey, cinnamon, cloves, and pepper in a blender. Cover with the lid and blend on high speed for about 1 minute or until mixture is liquefied.

2. Transfer the mixture to a small saucepan over high heat and heat until steaming, not boiling. If desired, use an immersion blender or an electric milk whisk to froth the mixture.

1 serving = 1 latte

DOSE: 1 Golden Latte provides 5 mg THC if you have used the Recommended Carrier Amounts table (page 9) to make the Canna Healing Honey.

>>>> Iced Golden Smoothie

Makes: 1 smoothie

1 cup coconut milk

½ cup frozen mango chunks

½ banana, cut into chunks

1 piece (1 inch) fresh turmeric, roughly chopped, or ½ teaspoon ground turmeric

1 piece (1 inch) fresh ginger, roughly chopped, or ½ teaspoon ground ginger

1 teaspoon Canna Coco Oil (page 13)

2 tablespoons evening primrose oil, optional (see Recipe Notes)

About 6 ice cubes (see Recipe Notes)

---

1 serving = 1 smoothie

DOSE: 1 Iced Golden Smoothie provides about 5 mg THC if you have used the Recommended Carrier Amounts table (page 9) to make the Canna Coco Oil.

— Combine the coconut milk, mango, banana, turmeric, ginger, Canna Coco Oil, evening primrose oil (if using), and ice in a blender. Blend on high speed for 30 seconds or until the turmeric and ginger are liquefied.

Recipe Notes

- The oil from evening primrose (*Oenothera biennis*) seeds is used internally or topically to decrease pain and swelling because it is high in GLA (gamma-linolenic acid), an omega-6 fatty acid also found in black currant (*Ribes nigrum*) as well as borage oil (*Borago officinalis*). See Resources (page 210).

- If you are taking Cannabis to help alleviate inflammation, consider making Ayurvedic Canna Butter (page 27) using grated fresh ginger, fresh or ground turmeric, and a teaspoon of freshly ground black pepper. You can use it in place of the turmeric, ginger, and Canna Coco Oil.

- Of course, you can omit the ice, if desired.

>>> Honey Yogurt Cooler

½ cup almond or regular milk

1 cup Greek-style plain yogurt

¼ cups raw almonds or pistachio nuts

¼ cup liquid honey

1 teaspoon Canna Honey (page 24)

1 sprig fresh mint, tulsi, or thyme, optional (see Recipe Note)

---

1 serving = 1 drink

DOSE: 1 Honey Yogurt Cooler provides about 5 mg THC if you have used the Recommended Carrier Amounts table (page 9) to make the Canna Honey.

— Combine the milk, yogurt, nuts, liquid honey, Canna Honey, and mint (if using) in a blender. Blend on high speed for 30 seconds or until the ingredients are liquefied.

Recipe Note

- Tulsi (*Ocimum tenuiflorum*), also known as holy basil, is a powerful healing herb. If you happen to be growing it, use it fresh in this recipe or dried in the teas.

>>> Pat's Root Beverage Blend

(a raw Cannabis recipe)

Makes: 2 cups, no THC

½ cup chopped fresh or dried Cannabis roots

½ cup chopped fresh or dried dandelion roots

½ cup chopped fresh or dried burdock roots

½ cup chopped fresh or dried chicory roots

2 tablespoons fresh or dried chopped licorice root

1 piece (2 inches) cinnamon stick, crushed into fine pieces

1. ***If you're using fresh roots:*** Scrub the roots, chop them in a food processor, measure, and spread them on a rimmed baking sheet. Roast in a preheated 300°F (150°C) oven for 45 minutes or until golden, stirring after 20 minutes. Reduce the oven temperature to 200°F (100°C) and roast for 1 more hour or until the roots are thoroughly dry, stirring every 30 minutes. Set aside to cool.
   If you're using dried roots: Spread the roots on a rimmed baking sheet and roast in a preheated 300°F (150°C) oven for 35 minutes or until golden, stirring every 10 minutes. Set aside to cool.

2. Combine the roasted roots with the cinnamon in a bowl and stir to mix well. Transfer to an airtight jar, label, and store in a cool, dark place.

Recipe Notes

- This makes a warming hot coffee–substitute drink (see Brewed Root Beverage below), but without the jitters from caffeine.

- See Resources (page 210) for online sources for the roots in this recipe and use your own Cannabis roots.

- Roasting the roots adds a richer taste, but is not absolutely necessary.

>>>> Brewed Root Beverage

(per cup of hot beverage)

Makes: 1 drink

¼ cup Pat's Root Beverage Blend (recipe above)

1 cup boiling water

1 teaspoon Canna Honey (page 24) or Canna Cream (page 21)

Milk and/or sugar, to taste, optional

— Grind the root blend to a fine or medium-size powder. Use 1 tablespoon ground roots for every cup of beverage. Brew as you would coffee in a drip coffeemaker or a French press. Add the Canna Honey and taste before adding milk and/or sugar, if desired.

1 serving = 1 drink

DOSE: **1 Brewed Root Beverage provides 5 mg THC if you have used the Recommended Carrier Amounts table (page 9) to make the Canna Honey.**

>>>> Power Herb Cocoa Blend

(a raw Cannabis recipe)

Makes: 1 cup, no THC

½ cup unsweetened dark cocoa powder

¼ cup ground power herb (choose one herb from Appendix B, page 186)

3 tablespoons coconut sugar

1 tablespoon ground cinnamon

2 teaspoons ground cardamom

— Whisk together the cocoa, power herb, sugar, cinnamon, and cardamom in a bowl. Transfer the mixture to a 1-cup Mason jar. Seal, label, and store in a cool, dark cupboard.

Recipe Note

• You can add 1 tablespoon of the Power Herb Cocoa Blend per serving to smoothies or juices.

>>>> Canna-Cocoa

(per cup of cocoa)

Makes: 1 cup

1 cup nondairy or regular milk

1 tablespoon Power Herb Cocoa Blend (recipe above, plus more as needed)

1 teaspoon Canna Oil (page 15) or Canna Cream (page 21)

1. Heat the milk in a saucepan over medium-high heat. When bubbles form around the inside of the pan, whisk in the Power Herb Cocoa Blend. Taste and add more of the cocoa blend, if desired.

2. Pour the cocoa into a mug and stir in the Canna Oil.

1 serving = 1 cup

DOSE: 1 teaspoon Canna Oil provides about 5 mg THC if you have used the Recommended Carrier Amounts table (page 9) to make it.

>>> Virgin Watermelon Sangria

Juice of 1 lime

4 cups cubed, seeded watermelon, divided

3 tablespoons granulated sugar

1 or 2 teaspoons Raspberry-Thyme Simple Syrup (page 38; see Recipe Note)

2 fresh thyme sprigs, for garnish

---

1 serving = 1 drink

DOSE: 1 teaspoon of Raspberry-Thyme Simple Syrup provides 5 mg THC if you have used the Recommended Carrier Amounts table (page 9) to make it.

---

1. Combine the lime juice and 2 cups of the watermelon in a blender and puree. Pour into a pitcher. Add the remaining watermelon, the sugar, and the Raspberry-Thyme Simple Syrup to the blender and blend.

2. Pour the second puree into the pitcher and whisk to mix well. Taste and add cold water to thin, if desired. Serve chilled and garnished with fresh thyme sprigs.

Recipe Note

- This recipe makes 2 drinks. You can add any flavor of Cannabis-infused simple syrup (pages 37–39) or Canna Honey (page 24) to it. Keep in mind that 1 teaspoon of Cannabis-infused syrup or honey is the appropriate dose for 1 drink.

TEAS TO EASE INTO SLEEP

Quality sleep (and getting enough of it) is crucial not only to health and wellness but to our very survival. When we can't sleep, when we can't reach the deep, REM (rapid eye movement) sleep cycles, or if our sleep is interrupted, we don't function at our best, we feel foggy, we can't concentrate or form new pathways to learning, and our emotions can drive our thoughts, making us reactive and impulsive, rather than thoughtful in our actions. It gets worse if we move into actual sleep deficiency. People who have chronic insomnia are at risk of developing some major chronic diseases, including heart and kidney disease, cardiovascular disease, depression, diabetes, and obesity.

Cannabis has been lauded for alleviating a long list of conditions, but, from my personal experience, sleep issues, inflammation, and pain are the disorders for which Cannabis benefits most people, most of the time. But not just any strain of Cannabis works best. It's widely known that indica-dominant strains that are high in CBD and CBN and relatively low (under 10 percent) in THC are the most sedative and pain-reducing.

We know that CBD and THC are not water-soluble, which is why I've used fats or high-fat ingredients to coax the medicinal cannabinoids from Cannabis for my infusions in chapter 1. For great sleep results, I recommend that you make a honey, oil, simple syrup, or tincture from that chapter (they're interchangeable in these recipes, so you only have to make one), follow my tips, and create the perfect nighttime nog from the teas here. If you're really serious about getting a good night's sleep, see Appendix B (page 200) for more tips on sleep and try adding at least one power herb from the list for sleep on pages 201–202 in Appendix B.

Tisane refers to an herbal tea (or infusion) made by pouring just-boiled water over fresh or dried herbs and steeping for three to five minutes. Tea made with black or green tea leaves (*Camellia sinensis*) is never called a tisane; it is simply referred to as "tea." It gets a bit confusing because a tisane (made with herbs) may be called an "herbal tea."

>>>> Bedtime Tea

(a loose tea blend)

Makes: 1¼ cups, no THC

½ cup dried lemon balm

½ cup finely chopped or ground dried valerian

¼ cup dried chamomile

¼ cup finely chopped or ground dried ashwagandha, optional (see Resources, page 210)

— Combine the lemon balm, valerian, chamomile, and ashwagandha (if using) in a 2-cup jar. Seal, label, and store in a cool, dark cupboard.

STEEPED BEDTIME TEA

(per cup of tea)

Makes: 1 cup

1 tablespoon Bedtime Tea blend (recipe above)

1 cup boiled water

1 teaspoon Canna Honey (page 24)

1 serving = 1 cup

DOSE: 1 cup of Steeped Bedtime Tea provides about 5 mg THC if you have used the Recommended Carrier Amounts table (page 9) to make the Canna Honey.

1. Measure the tea blend into a small teapot or heatproof jar with a lid. Pour the boiled water over the tea blend. Cover and let steep for 5 minutes.

2. Strain the steeped tea through a fine-mesh strainer into a cup or a small glass and stir in the Canna Honey. Drink immediately or cover and chill (out of the reach of children).

Recipe Notes

- Since the THC is in the Canna Honey you add to the tea, if you prefer not to drink a full cup of tea before bedtime, you can make the tea using a much smaller amount of boiled water (¼ or ½ cup) and still get the full dose of THC.

- Of course, you can add more regular non-Cannabis honey to taste.

- THC isn't water-soluble, so always add a dose of Canna Honey (page 24), Canna Oil (page 15), Cannabis-infused simple syrup (pages 36–39), or Canna Tincture (pages 33–34) to impart the medicinal or psychoactive cannabinoids to the tea.

Honey Lemon Ginger Tea

Makes: 4 cups

4 cups water

1 piece (3 inches) fresh ginger, peeled and coarsely chopped

Juice of 1 lemon

About 3 tablespoons liquid honey, plus more to taste

1 teaspoon Canna Honey (page 24) per consenting adult

4 thin slices lemon, for garnish

1 serving = 1 cup

DOSE: 1 teaspoon Canna Honey provides 5 mg THC if you have used the Recommended Carrier Amounts table (page 9) to make it.

1. Bring the water to a boil in a saucepan over high heat. Add the ginger, cover the pan, reduce the heat to medium-low, and simmer for 10 minutes.

2. Stir in the lemon juice and liquid honey and stir to dissolve. Taste and add more honey, if desired.

3. Strain the tea into 4 warmed cups. Add 1 teaspoon Canna Honey for people who wish to have it. Garnish with lemon slices.

Soothing Tea Blend

(a loose tea blend)

Makes: ½ cup, no THC

¼ cup dried chamomile flowers, crushed

¼ cup dried milky oats, crushed

2 tablespoons dried skullcap (optional)

— Combine the chamomile, oats, and skullcap (if using) in a 1-cup jar. Seal and shake well. Label the jar, and store it in a cool, dry, dark cupboard.

STEEPED SOOTHING TEA

(per cup of tea)

Makes: 1 cup

1 tablespoon Soothing Tea Blend (recipe above)

1 cup boiled water

1 teaspoon Canna Honey (page 24), Canna Oil (page 15), or Canna Tincture (pages 33–34)

1 serving = 1 cup

DOSE: 1 cup of Steeped Soothing Tea provides 5 mg THC if you have used the Recommended Carrier Amounts table (page 9) to make the Canna Honey.

1. Crush the tea blend between the palms of your hands and place it in a small teapot or heatproof jar with a lid. Pour the boiled water on top. Cover and let the tea steep for 5 minutes.

2. Using a fine-mesh strainer, strain the steeped tea into a cup or a small glass and stir in the Canna Honey. Drink immediately or cover and cool slightly, out of the reach of children.

Recipe Notes

- THC isn't water-soluble so always add a dose of Canna Oil (page 15), Canna Honey (page 24), Cannabis-infused simple syrup (pages 36–39), or Canna Tincture (pages 33–34) to impart the medicinal or psychoactive compounds to the tea.

- *To make a pot of tea:* Spoon 6 to 8 tablespoons of Soothing Tea Blend into a teapot and cover with 4 to 6 cups of boiling water. Cover and steep for 5 minutes. Strain the steeped tea into 4 or 6 cups and add 1 teaspoon Canna Honey for people who wish to have it.

- *To make iced tea:* Make a pot of tea using 6 to 8 tablespoons of Soothing Tea Blend and follow the directions above. Set the tea aside to cool and store in the refrigerator in an airtight container. Pour into glasses filled with ice. Add 1 teaspoon Canna Honey for people who wish to have it.

- You can also add 1 tablespoon of the Soothing Tea Blend to a smoothie or juice.

< Cannabis Basics: >
Understanding the Human Endocannabinoid System

Cannabinoids are the chemical compounds found in all parts of the Cannabis plant, most of which are concentrated in the female flower. Along with the psychedelic THC, arguably the most famous of all the cannabinoids, these compounds are also the healing elements that provide relief for an array of mental, emotional, and physical symptoms. Research is ongoing, but it is currently thought that there are around 113 known cannabinoids found in Cannabis. Some cannabinoids, such as CBN, are helpful in easing anxiety and pain, while others, specifically CBC, are effective at reducing inflammation. This is why I recommend that you use the whole flower (or plant) for medicine and food.

What many people may be surprised to learn is that our bodies actually produce cannabinoids, and those cannabinoids are called endocannabinoids. The role of endocannabinoids in the body is to maintain homeostasis or balance; hence, they regulate internal stability and health by activating specific receptors found concentrated in the brain and in smaller numbers all over the body. The endocannabinoid system (ECS) is the largest receptor system in the body, affecting appetite, digestive processes, sleep, immunity, inflammation, memory, mood, stress, the nervous system, metabolism, and temperature.

Cannabinoids from Cannabis imitate the body's own endocannabinoids by binding to the body's receptors. In fact, as fatty acid–based *keys*, they fit into the body's own receptors that are the *locks* (or gateways) to the body's endocannabinoid system. Different cannabinoids have different effects because they bind to different receptors. For example, THC binds to CB1 receptors in the brain, which is why we feel euphoric when THC is introduced by smoking or in food. We get no high from CBD because it doesn't bind to CB1 receptors.

Using Cannabis medicinally is appropriate when our own ECS is deficient or not working optimally or when we are under stress. Finding a strain

< 182 >

and ratio of THC to CBD that works for your health is a bonus of making your own edibles. I've made it easy for you to gauge your THC tolerance with "Your First Cannabis Edibles Test" (page 18) and if you use my log to record details (page 10), you'll get very good at determining your preference for sativa- or indica-dominant strains as well as the ratio of CBD to THC that works best for your needs.

PLANT SPECIES: *Cannabis sativa, Cannabis indica*, and *Cannabis ruderalis*

The genus *Cannabis* likely originated in wet habitats of the Asiatic continent. Due to its amazing uses (as food, for textiles, as medicine, and as a psychoactive substance), it was one of the first plants to be domesticated. Although the German botanist Leonart Fuchs was the first to call domesticated hemp *sativa*, it was Carl Linnaeus, Europe's quintessential botanist and taxonomy specialist of the 18th century, who named the species of Euorpean hemp plants *Cannabis sativa* or *C. indica*. In botanic organization, the first word in the name, in this case *Cannabis*, indicates the genus. This word in the name is always capitalized. The next, uncapitalized word(s) in the name, in this case, *sativa* or *indica*, indicates a species or variety in the *Cannabis* genus. Cannabis is categorized in the Cannabacease family.

Sometime after Linnaeus, French naturalist Jean-Baptiste Lamarck was given psychoactive varieties of Cannabis from India and, because they showed differences from Linnaeus's *Cannabis sativa*, he named those specimens *Cannabis indica*.

Another variety, *Cannabis ruderalis*, was thought to be a different species by D. E. Janischewsky, a Russian who observed it in south-central Russia.

Plants in this category are typically higher in CBD with very little THC.

Most botanists and people in the Cannabis industry now believe that wild species have all but disappeared and that pure *C. indica*, *C. sativa*, and *C. ruderalis* plants and strains no longer exist. This means that almost all Cannabis plants are hybrids now, which is why I use the terms *sativa-dominant* or *indica-dominant* to indicate the predominant qualities of a particular strain.

Cannabis indica plants are stout with broad-fingered leaves, and their buds and flowers are denser; they actually weigh more than those on a *C. sativa* plant. Indica-dominant strains are thought to deliver calming and sedative effects, centered mostly in the body. They relieve pain, induce sleep, and help to relieve anxiety. Generally, indica strains are suited to evening, specifically bedtime use, or for pain, if rest is prescribed.

You can easily spot the taller *C. sativa* plant with its long, thin-fingered leaves, and you will likely feel its effects as being uplifting, stimulating, creative, more cerebral and euphoric, or intoxicating. Typically, sativa strains work best in daytime and for evening social settings.

Cannabis sativa

Cannabis indica

Cannabis for Symptom Relief

ANXIETY

Anxiety is rampant in our society, whether we call it stress, mental exhaustion, emotional or physical burnout, tension, panic, or feeling overwhelmed. Many people are turning to Cannabis to help manage anxiety, no matter what the cause. At the same time, they are practicing calming techniques such as yoga, deep breathing, meditation, and mindfulness. So, while CBD-rich Cannabis edibles can complement and support these and other practices in the short term, there needs to be more research on whether Cannabis can maintain reduction of symptoms in the long term. I recommend trying microdosing (see page 11) and closely monitoring your response. Developing long-term, behavior-based coping strategies may also prove to be rewarding. **CAUTION:** Young adults (under 25) and people who are prone to depression should avoid THC completely; see "Risks of Early Cannabis Use" (page vii).

Recommended Ratio

Anecdotal evidence points to the effectiveness of *C. indica* to treat anxiety, since most people prefer to relax the mind rather than supercharge it, so high-CBD oil (over 15 percent) with low THC (6 percent or less) or a whole flower Cannabis strain with the same ratio is recommended for anxiety. If possible, look for high levels of the terpene myrcene in the strain.

Recommended Foods

- Choose foods high in B_9, folate, B_{12}, and cobalamin, such as asparagus, dark leafy greens, broccoli, Brussels sprouts, citrus fruits, beans, peas, lentils, sunflower seeds, and avocado. These vitamins work together to structure and maintain the myelin surrounding nerve cells and help prevent depression, confusion, dementia, and poor memory. The green vegetables are also high

< 186 >

in magnesium, which helps regulate cortisol levels and promotes feelings of wellness.

- New research suggests that anti-inflammatory foods (see page 68) and treatment help alleviate symptoms of depression in some people.
- Whole grains, nuts, and seeds (sunflower seeds, peanuts, flaxseeds, almonds) are a good source of folate as well as B vitamins, which help to keep nerves and brain cells healthy.
- Antioxidants and vitamin C repair and protect cells from the ravaging effects of stress. Blueberries and other dark-colored fruits and vegetables are all good sources of antioxidants and vitamin C (see "Anti-Inflammatory Foods," page 68).
- Foods high in vitamin C, such as guava, black currants, red peppers, strawberries, citrus fruit, and sea buckthorn berries lower blood pressure and the stress hormone cortisol.
- Avocados and other omega-3 fatty acid–rich foods (and oils), such as almonds, walnuts, flaxseeds, and fatty fish, such as salmon, mackerel, and sardines, help keep cortisol and adrenaline from spiking when you are anxious.
- Turkey, quinoa, spirulina, and organic soy products are rich in tryptophan, the amino acid that signals the brain to release the feel-good, calming chemical serotonin.
- Oatmeal has a calming effect.
- Dark chocolate (a minimum of 70 percent cacao) is shown to increase levels of the neurotransmitters serotonin and dopamine, brain chemicals associated with feelings of pleasure.

Foods to Avoid

- Avoid caffeine. Caffeine is a stimulant found in cola drinks, coffee, green and black tea, and chocolate, among other things.
- Eliminate artificial and refined sugars (especially aspartame) found in diet soda, processed food, and drinks—they inhibit the body's ability to cope with stress.
- Avoid processed and fried foods, due to their high amounts of artificial and refined sugars, low-quality fats, gluten, preservatives, and other additives.
- Be mindful that alcohol is a depressant.

Recommended Herbs to Treat Anxiety

In general, earth-energy (adaptogen) herbs help to connect you to the deep energy reserves within your body, and they work to balance stress to bring you to equilibrium. Some of these types of herbs include the following in order of their importance to easing anxiety:

- Reishi (*Ganoderma* spp.) is a mushroom that helps us adapt to and handle stress.
- Ashwagandha (*Withania somnifera*) is an excellent herb for the totally burned-out body. It replenishes vitality and strength, builds reserves, and helps us sleep through stressful times. Add it to the Canna Tincture (pages 33–34).

- Chamomile (*Matricaria recutita*) is a traditional sedative that is also safe for children. It is most commonly taken as a tea for insomnia. It also eases restlessness and irritability. Blue chamomile essential oil can be added to a nighttime bath to soothe nerves.
- Kava kava (*Piper methysticum*) appears to be the best herbal treatment for anxiety, but should only be used for short periods (a few days or one week at the most).
- Lemon balm (*Melissa officinalis*) relieves restlessness, nervous tension, digestive and gastrointestinal disorders, and calms the nervous system. It is also safe for children.
- Milky oats (*Avena* spp.) is nerve tonic that soothes, relaxes, strengthens, calms, centers, and grounds us.
- Passionflower (*Passiflora* spp.) not only helps ease anxiety but also alleviates anxiety-related insomnia.
- Skullcap (*Scutellaria lateriflora*) soothes muscle tension and the nervous system. It also lowers inflammation, regulates sleep, balances hormones, and eases anxiety.
- Valerian (*Valeriana officinalis*) relaxes us and helps us sleep.

ANXIETY POWER HERB:
Rose (*Rosa* spp.)

Not just a pretty herb, rose works to bring deep and sometimes strong emotions to the surface so that they can be released and the body can relax and repair. Herbalist Rebecca Altman (Kings Road Apothecary; see Resources, page 210) says, "Wild rose softens the areas that we tense to protect ourselves, unraveling emotional tension patterns that get locked in the body." Rose works well with Cannabis, but be aware of its ability to release old trauma and tension. I have included rose and lavender essential oils in the CBD-Spiked Relax Spa Scrub (page 99).

APPETITE LOSS

The munchies are not a figment of a Cannabis-induced imagination. We definitely do crave sweet snacks because THC stimulates the release of dopamine in our brain, which increases our sensory affinity for food. For people who are concerned about weight gain, the good news is that CBD mitigates our cravings, and a ratio of around 13 percent CBD to 10 percent or less THC actually helps to suppress appetite.

The thought of having little or no appetite may seem strange, or it may even be a secret desire for some people, but, for many, it is just as much a curse as having a burning desire to constantly eat. Known as anorexia, the condition manifests in patients with cancer or AIDS, the elderly, or others who simply do not find food interesting or who don't have someone with whom to share a meal, or who don't taste the rich flavors in food as they once might have. In extreme cases, where mental conditions cause anorexia, the condition is known as anorexia nervosa. No matter how or why the condition afflicts a person, loss of appetite can be serious, leading to malnutrition and, in some cases, death.

Recommended Ratio

Look for an indica strain that is almost balanced in the CBD to THC ratio, with CBD from 9 to 13 percent, with CBN if possible, and THC from 6 to 10 percent.

Recommended Foods

If you're not eating much, when you do eat, choose nutrient-rich foods, high in protein (fish, chicken, beef, lamb, eggs, hummus, peas, beans, legumes, cheese, nuts, and nut butters) and high-quality fats; whole grains; fresh fruit, such as avocados and bananas; dried fruit; and vegetables, such as sweet potatoes, peas, beans, and corn, rather than high-salt or high-sugar foods or beverages with few or no nutrients. Nutrient-dense foods, even if eaten in small amounts, deliver the energy and essential components for a healthy body, mind, and spirit.

Try to always eat breakfast, and eat lots of smaller meals throughout the day or snacks, such as smoothies with nuts and full-fat yogurt to power up.

Foods to Avoid

Give junk foods, fried foods, and processed foods a pass because you want to consume high-quality nutrients that nourish your cells, not empty calories.

Appetite-Stimulating Herbs

Bitter Herbs

Bitter herbs trigger taste buds at the back of the tongue to signal the central nervous system to stimulate the flow of digestive juices from the mouth, the stomach, the pancreas, the duodenum, the gallbladder, and the liver. In other words, they get the digestive tract working.

Try drinking ¼ cup of an IPA beer or eating a small arugula and/or dandelion leaf salad before dinner. Make the Canna Tincture (pages 33–34) using one of the following bitter herbs, and take 1 teaspoon 20 minutes before eating:

— Artichoke (*Cynara scolymus*)
— Astragalus (*Astragalus membranaceus*)—if you are not eating due to chemotherapy treatment
— Barberry root (*Berberis vulgaris*)
— Dandelion (*Taraxacum officinale*)
— Ginger (*Zingiber officinale*)—to relieve feelings of nausea
— Hops (*Humulus lupulus*)

Carminative Herbs

Carminative herbs warm and soothe the digestive tract and increase the effectiveness of digestion so your body gets the most nutrients from the food you consume. Sip a tea made with carminative herbs with your meal and include carminative herbs in smoothies, tea blends, and other recipes found in this book, such as Baked Vegetable Chips (page 112) or Ginger Bites (page 62). Examples include:

– Cardamom (*Elettaria cardamomum*)
– Cumin (*Cuminum cyminum*)
– Fennel (*Foeniculum vulgare*)
– Lemon balm (*Melissa officinalis*)

APPETITE POWER HERB: Gentian (*Gentiana lutea*)

Gentian is a popular digestive bitter that has been included in traditional "bitters" concoctions since before the turn of the 19th century. Consuming an ounce (2 tablespoons) of a bitter herbal digestif (before a meal) or an aperitif (after a meal) will help to reduce gas, bloating, symptoms of food allergies, and indigestion. You can make a tincture with Cannabis and gentian using the Canna Tincture recipes on pages 33–34.

ATHLETICS

While it's strictly illegal for professionals to compete with Cannabis in their system, some athletes have discovered that taking Cannabis during training or when they're injured can help improve performance and healing. Because it increases sensory awareness, Cannabis is helpful during training when the mind-muscle connections are being wired and fired in the brain. Cannabis is also helpful in staying focused. Sativa strains are most often used in pre-event training and microdosing (page 11) may be as effective as taking a regular dose.

Cannabis is also helpful for treating stress and insomnia, two of the lingering issues from concussion. For treating pain, Cannabis is instrumental during the recovery period, and indica strains are best in this case.

CAUTIONS: Cannabis can be detected in blood and urine for 30 days or longer, and it shows up in hair samples months after smoking or eating it. Since smoking severely damages the lungs, Cannabis edibles or drinkables are the way to go for most people, and especially for athletes.

Recommended Ratio

– *Preworkout and during training competition:* Sativa strains typically deliver an energizing high. Start experimenting with sativa strains that are only slightly higher in THC (around 10 to 12 percent) to CBD (6 to 8 percent).
– *For recovery:* Indica strains are sedating and may help you relax to heal. Try indica strains that are higher in CBD (9 to 15 percent) to THC (6 to 12 percent).

— *For concussion:* Anecdotal evidence points to CBD oil or flowers high in CBD with minimal THC.

Recommended Foods

— Carbohydrate intake is important for all levels of activity, but if you train or perform for more than 90 minutes, you may want to do some basic research about "carbohydrate loading," a technique that calls for eating foods that provide 70 percent of their calories from carbohydrates (pasta, bread, sugars from fruits and vegetables).

— Choose dark-colored fruits and vegetables because they are high in anti-inflammatory, antioxidant anthocyanins that help prevent oxidative stress from extreme physical exertion. Eat blueberries; kale and other dark leafy greens; red and green peppers; broccoli, purple cabbage, and other cruciferous vegetables; tomatoes; red, black, and blue berries; black plums; and black cherries. Drink tart cherry juice just before and after training or for a week prior to intense activity.

— Enjoy quinoa at least once a week! Quinoa was a power food for the ancient Incas because it contains almost twice the amount of protein as other grains, and that protein has all nine essential amino acids for building muscle.

— Include omega-3 fatty acid–rich foods in your daily diet, such as almonds and walnuts (and their butters), flaxseeds, and fatty fish (wild salmon, mackerel, sardines), because they help reduce inflammation.

— Include lentils, peas, and all varieties of beans (black, soy, white, pinto, kidney) as part of your daily diet. Their fat is unsaturated, and they are an excellent source of fiber and plant protein. Note that if legumes are new to your diet, you should introduce them slowly and avoid eating them the night before an athletic event or performance because the fiber may contribute to gastrointestinal distress.

— Bananas contain about 420 mg of potassium each, which is essential for preventing muscle cramps and spasms.

Foods to Avoid

Empty-calorie foods, processed foods, fried foods, and saturated fats all add to your caloric intake without supplying any nutrients.

Herbs for Enhanced Athletic Performance

Adaptogens are balancers, and they help the body respond to stress. They build energy reserves and generally help the body adapt to and recover from rigorous workouts, training, and endurance activities. The following adaptogens are worth including in tinctures, drinks, and other edibles in this book.

- Ashwagandha (*Withania somnifera*) increases cardiorespiratory response and helps the body maintain a healthy balance while under physical stress. It also lessens recovery time from sports injuries.
- Maca (*Lepidium meyenii*) is a cruciferous, turnip-like plant, native to South America, that grows at high elevations (13,000-plus feet). As an adaptogen, it has the potential to recharge fatigued adrenal glands and help you respond to stress. Especially important for sports training as well as injuries, it aids in muscle tissue recovery and increases stamina and energy. Several types are available; see Resources (page 210).
- Rhodiola (*Rhodiola rosea*) grows at high altitudes in the arctic areas of Europe and Asia, and rhodiola's traditional and scientific use is well-documented in Sweden, Norway, Iceland, Germany, and Russia. Studies point to the effectiveness of the plant's roots in helping prevent fatigue, stress, and the ravages of oxygen deprivation. Dried, chopped rhodiola root, as well as tinctures, are available; see Resources (page 210).
- Schisandra (*Schisandra chinensis*) is often called a superberry, and it has been shown to have many benefits. But because it improves cardiovascular health, combats stress, and increases energy, it is often recommended for use by athletes.
- Siberian ginseng (*Eleutherococcus senticosus*) makes an excellent overall tonic to enhance athletic performance, and it supports the body when under stress.
- Turmeric (*Curcuma longa*) is anti-

ATHLETICS POWER HERB:
Hawthorn (*Crataegus* spp.)

Hawthorn is a small tree or shrub that is commonly found throughout the northern hemisphere. It is said that hawthorn feeds the heart energetically by helping us open up to love, but quite literally it is also physically nourishing and toning, and protects the heart from potential damage. Because an extract of hawthorn increases both the force and the rate of blood flowing to the heart muscle, it increases cardiac performance and output without actually making the heart work harder (in fact, it reduces the heart's workload). Perhaps most important to athletes is hawthorn's ability to increase the heart's tolerance for oxygen deficiency. The recommended dose of hawthorn tincture is 2 to 4 dropperfuls, morning and evening. According to Christopher Hobbs, PhD, hawthorn is safe for long-term use and safe with drugs such as digoxin. Include hawthorn berries, flowers, and leaves (see Resources, page 210) in the Canna Tincture (pages 33–34) or try adding it to teas or smoothies.

inflammatory (see "Deflating Inflammation, page 68); use fresh or powdered.

- Valerian (*Valeriana officinalis*) can help if sleep is an issue, and some athletes have found an extract or tincture of valerian root helpful as a muscle relaxant.

EPILEPSY

Epilepsy is defined as recurrent seizures that occur because of a sudden jolt of electrical activity in the brain, and it is one of the most common neurological conditions from which people suffer. Whole-spectrum CBD has been shown to be valuable in controlling seizures in some people, especially for people unresponsive to other treatments. Perhaps the most widely known case of CBD halting grand mal seizures is that of Charlotte Figi, who was helped by a strain named in her honor, Charlotte's Web. The Charlotte's Web strain is indica-dominant, and the CBD content can be as high as 20 percent, with so little THC that no high is experienced.

While more research is required, it may be safe to say that other neurological disorders, including multiple sclerosis, post-traumatic stress disorder, Parkinson's, and ALS (aka Lou Gehrig's disease) may also benefit from a high CBD (28 percent) to extremely low (1 percent) THC Cannabis strain.

Recommended Ratio

Anecdotal evidence points to the effectiveness of an indica strain that is high CBD (over 15 percent CBD) and with a very low amount of THC (5 percent or less, 1 percent for children or young adults). Look for a strain with significant amounts of THCV, if possible.

Recommended Foods

- The ketogenic diet, with its high-fat, low-carbohydrate components, has been used since the early 20th century as a treatment for epilepsy in children. It may be beneficial for you to investigate it and follow it carefully.
- High-quality fats, such as avocado oil, coconut oil, olive oil, butter, cream, nut butters, and omega-3 fatty acid–rich foods, such as almonds, walnuts, flaxseeds, and fatty fish (salmon, mackerel, sardines), may help to control seizures in some people.
- Carbohydrates may cause energy peaks and slumps, so eliminate white bread, sugars, baked goods, high-sugar drinks, and fruit juices and try incorporating small amounts of fresh raw fruits and vegetables low on the glycemic index, and small amounts of whole grains, such as quinoa, amaranth, spelt, and whole wheat berries, in your diet.
- Protein from organic lamb and chicken, and foods high in vitamin D, such as wild-caught salmon or mackerel, egg yolks, shiitake

mushrooms, legumes, beans, peas, and nuts, are important because they offer high-quality protein to nourish the brain and body.

— Researchers have found that people in a state of epilepsy show a deficiency of magnesium in the blood, so eat magnesium-rich foods, such as legumes, broccoli, squash, leafy-green vegetables; seeds (such as sunflower and pumpkin); and nuts (especially almonds, walnuts, pecans) every day.

Foods to Avoid

— Foods high in carbohydrates should be avoided, including potatoes, parsnips, beets, and other high-sugar vegetables; white bread, pasta, and rice; baked goods (cookies, cakes, biscuits); sugar (including honey, syrups, soda and juice drinks, and dates); high-sugar fruits (such as watermelon, grapes, bananas, and dried or overripe fruit).

— Processed, fried, and junk foods are definite no-nos.

Herbs for Healthy Muscle and Nerve Function

Magnesium is a key nutrient for keeping healthy muscle and nerve function in the body. Since magnesium is the main element of chlorophyll, which gives herbs (and plants) their green color, most green herbs will help boost magnesium in foods and drinks, especially the following herbs, which provide over 200 mg magnesium per ounce (listed in order of highest to lowest in magnesium):

— Stinging Nettle (*Urtica dioica*)
— Dill (*Anethum graveolens*)
— Basil (*Ocimum basilicum*), especially holy basil (*O. tenuiflorum*)
— Thyme (*Thymus* spp.)
— Parsley (*Petroselinum*)

CAUTION: Mixing herbs with drugs can cause serious reactions. If you are taking antiseizure drugs, avoid ginkgo (*Ginkgo biloba*) and St. John's wort (*Hypericum perforatum*), and consult with your health-care provider on the use of Cannabis.

INFLAMMATION

As noted on page 68, inflammation is a natural response, but if it becomes chronic, it can lead to some very severe diseases, including some cancers and rheumatoid arthritis. I can't emphasize enough the anti-inflammatory properties of THCA, which means that you can take Cannabis in the raw, fresh, or dried state (undecarboxylated)

and get the relief you need without the high when THC is ingested.

Studies show that, generally speaking, CBD exerts potent anti-inflammatory and antioxidant effects. Low doses of THC have been shown to inhibit atherosclerosis, a chronic inflammatory disease.

Recommended Ratio

Experiment with an indica strain that is high in CBD (and CBN, if possible), with between 3 percent and 7 percent THC. If your medical Cannabis supplier has tested for some of the flavonoids and other cannabinoids, try to find a strain that is a good source of luteolin, THCA, CBG, CBC, and CBDA.

Recommended Foods

– Try to live on dark-colored fruits and vegetables because they are high in anti-inflammatory, antioxidant anthocyanins that help prevent oxidative stress from extreme physical exertion. Eat blueberries; kale and other dark leafy greens; red and green peppers; broccoli, purple cabbage, and other cruciferous vegetables; tomatoes; red, black, and blue berries; black plums; and black cherries.

– Pineapple makes for a good treat due to the bromelain, an enzyme that assists digestion and is anti-inflammatory.

– Eat omega-3 fatty acid–rich foods, such as almonds, walnuts, flaxseeds, and fatty fish (wild salmon, mackerel, sardines), because they help reduce inflammation.

– Matcha is a powder made from a high grade of unfermented green tea leaves. It's high in antioxidants but contains caffeine. To make traditional matcha, combine 1 teaspoon matcha powder with ⅓ cup boiled water in a small teacup. Whisk to a froth using a small whisk or a bamboo brush.

– Shiitake mushrooms contain the amino acid ergothioneine, which inhibits oxidative stress and may reduce inflammation.

Foods to Avoid

– Dairy can exacerbate inflammation—use nondairy milk and limit your intake of cheese.

– Stay away from fried and refined foods, red meats, saturated fat, and foods with gluten.

Anti-Inflammatory Herbs

– Turmeric (*Curcuma longa*). It's first in line because it is the most effective. Use fresh or powdered turmeric because research shows that it is effective in treating arthritis and osteoarthritis. Make Canna Curry Spice Paste (page 41) and use it in savory dishes.

– Cinnamon (*Cinnamomum* spp.). It's loaded with anti-inflammatory compounds such as cinnamaldehyde, a proven protein inhibitor.

– Cloves (*Syzygium aromaticum*). The eugenol in cloves inhibits an inflammation-causing enzyme, making it an effective anti-inflammatory herb.

– Ginger (*Zingiber officinalis*). This one is best fresh, but ground ginger can offer some relief. Gingerol and zingerone are being studied as the key to ginger's ability to reduce inflammation.

– Sage (*Salvia officinalis*). Carnosic acid and carnosol in sage help remove the free radical superoxide, which is an inflammation-causing compound.

- Black peppercorns (*Piper nigrum*). While they're not specifically anti-inflammatory, black peppercorns aid the body in healing osteo- and rheumatoid arthritis and boost the efficiency of turmeric.

ANTI-INFLAMMATORY POWER HERB:
Mullein (*Verbascum thapsus*)

Commonly seen at the edges of fields and unkempt yards, mullein is easily found in the wild or obtained online (see Resources, page 210). The root is used by herbalists to support the sacroiliac joint (at the pelvis) and the spine; lubricate other joints and ligaments; align bones, such as those in the knees, hips, and shoulders; and repair soft tissue. Mullein root gets us back in line. I recommend using it in the Joint Pain Relief Body Rub (page 73), along with a CBD-rich *Cannabis indica* strain.

MEMORY

Low doses of THC can improve the cognitive function in middle-aged humans and the elderly. It seems that it assists the neurons in the hippocampus section of the brain to sprout more synaptic connections (synapses bridge the gaps between the trillions of cells in our brain). High doses of CBD help protect against memory impairment and improve concentration and focus.
CAUTION: THC in Cannabis can have adverse effects on people under the age of 25. See "Risks of Early Cannabis Use" (page vii).

Recommended Ratio

You could start with a sativa strain that is higher in CBD (9 to 13 percent) and lower in THC (3 to 9 percent).

Recommended Foods

- Omega-3 fatty acid–rich foods, such as almonds, walnuts, flaxseeds, and fatty fish (wild salmon, mackerel, sardines), are the best foods to eat for cognitive health because the brain is made up of structural and functional fats essential for protecting the cells and assisting with communication between cells.
- Eat foods high in B_9, folate, B_{12}, and cobalamin, such as asparagus, dark leafy greens, broccoli, Brussels sprouts, citrus fruits, beans, peas, lentils, sunflower seeds, and avocado. These vitamins work together to structure and maintain the myelin sheath surrounding nerve cells and help prevent depression, confusion,

dementia, and poor memory. The dark green vegetables are also high in magnesium, which helps regulate cortisol levels and promotes feelings of wellness.

– Mushrooms, such as shiitake (*Lentinula edodes*) and maitake (*Grifola frondosa*), are good for you, but lion's mane (*Hericium erinaceus*), a particularly tasty North American native, has been shown to prevent inflammation and increase gray matter in the brain. In January 2017, the *Journal of Medicinal Food* reported that mushrooms may protect against Alzheimer's disease and other forms of dementia. (Try the Egg and Shiitake Mushroom Popovers on page 121 and substitute lion's mane mushrooms, if available.)

– Antioxidants and vitamin C repair and protect cells from the ravaging effects of stress. Eat blueberries, pomegranate, and other dark fruits and vegetables.

– Foods high in the fat-soluble vitamin K and choline, such as broccoli, dark leafy greens, asparagus, Brussels sprouts, and fish including seafood and especially fatty-fish such as salmon, bluefin tuna, sardines, and herring, help keep memory sharp by improving the flow of blood to the brain.

Foods to Avoid

Avoid processed and fried foods (just in case you forgot). They contain high amounts of artificial and refined sugars, low-quality fats, gluten, preservatives, and other additives.

Memory-Boosting Herbs

– Ashwagandha (*Withania somnifera*). Take it for stress and because it also helps protect against brain cell deterioration. It helps improve mental clarity and cognitive function.

– Gingko (*Gingko biloba*). Gingko improves blood circulation in the central nervous system, allowing oxygen to promote overall brain function. It has been shown in studies to improve memory and thought processes by protecting the nerve cells in the brain from damage brought on by dementia and Alzheimer's disease.

– Ginseng (*Eleutherococcus senticosus*). Ginseng has been shown to improve neurotransmitter activity that enhances memory.

– Rhodiola (*Rhodiola rosea*). As a powerful adaptogen, rhodiola stimulates the central nervous system and improves concentration, focus, and memory.

– Rosemary (*Rosmarinus officinalis*). Rosemary is a powerful antioxidant. Its carnosic acid can protect the brain from stroke and neurodegeneration (loss of structure or function of neurons that causes inability to transmit information to other nerve cells in the brain) that comes from toxins and free radicals.

MEMORY POWER HERB:
Gotu Kola (*Centella asiatica*)

Known for its rejuvenating properties, this small, creeping tropical perennial is used to protect against age-related memory loss, stress, and nervous disorders, such as Parkinson's disease. It is a blood tonic; it strengthens adrenal glands and relaxes the central nervous system. Add gotu kola to the alcohol tincture or the glycerine tincture on pages 33–34.

CAUTION: Do not use gotu kola if you are pregnant or suffer from epilepsy. Do not use it for longer than six weeks without a break.

PAIN

Pain is associated with every illness, acute and chronic, and there are a number of different kinds of pain, including somatic, visceral, and neuropathic—and subsets within each one. Whether you use raw Cannabis or decarboxylated Cannabis to treat pain, evidence suggests that cannabinoids are useful in pain reduction by inhibiting neuronal transmission in pain pathways. It is also noted that whole-spectrum THC and CBD are more effective than isolated THC or CBD.

The big news in pain and inflammation is the growing evidence that shows how Cannabis is reducing not only opioid use, but also the consumption of other liver-destroying prescription painkillers. A study by researchers at the University of Massachusetts and Colorado State University links the availability of adult-use Cannabis to a decrease of between 20 percent and 35 percent in deaths from opioid overdose.

Recommended Ratio

You will need to be your own research subject to determine what works best for your particular pain. Some people report better results from indica strains; others find sativa strains are better for relief from migraines, pain, and nausea. According to Dr. Barth Wilsey in his paper on neuropathic pain ("A Randomized, Placebo Controlled Cross-Over Trial of Cannabis Cigarettes in Neuropathic Pain," *Journal of Pain*, June 2008), low doses are just as effective as medium ones. I suggest starting out with an even ratio of CBD to THC, or perhaps one that is slightly higher in CBD. If possible, find a strain with CBN and CBC.

Recommended Foods

- Gamma-linolenic acid (GLA)–rich oils from currant (*Ribes nigrum*) and borage (*Borago officinalis*) seeds contain up to 25 percent

GLA, which reduces inflammation, curbs rheumatoid arthritic pain, and relieves morning stiffness and joint tenderness.

- Fresh fruits and vegetables (all colors), preferably raw, whole, or juiced—or steamed or gently cooked—should be eaten in abundance every day. Specifically, turn to dark-colored produce, such as blueberries, kale, and other dark leafy greens; red and green peppers; broccoli, purple cabbage, and other cruciferous vegetables; tomatoes; red, black, and blue berries; cherries, black plums, and cranberries.

- Some pain issues (such as arthritis and back, knee, and neck pain) are associated with chronic inflammation, so foods and herbs that help reduce inflammation are recommended (see page 195 and "Deflating Inflammation" page 68).

- Eat omega-3 fatty acid–rich foods, such as almonds, walnuts, flaxseeds, and fatty fish (wild salmon, mackerel, sardines) because they help reduce inflammation.

- Replace dairy and red meat proteins with tofu, tempeh, and other fermented forms of organic whole soy (miso or tamari, but not soy protein isolates commonly used in processed foods).

Foods to Avoid

- Avoid dairy due to its inflammatory tendencies—use nondairy milk and limit your intake of cheese. Similarly, fried and refined foods, saturated fats, and gluten are no-nos.

- All red meats should be off the menu.

Analgesic Herbs to Alleviate Pain

- Cayenne (*Capsicum* spp.) and fresh stinging nettle (*Urtica dioica*). Often used topically as an irritant to bring warmth and tingling to an area and internally for their pain-relieving endorphins.

- Devil's claw (*Harpagophytum procumbens*). Roots taken as a tea, extract, or tincture ease muscular tension or pain in the back, shoulders, and neck.

- Evening primrose (*Oenothera biennis*). Seeds are a good source of the amino acid tryptophan, shown to reduce pain caused by acute and chronic illness. The oil is available from Mountain Rose Herbs (see Resources on page 210).

- Ginseng (*Panax quinquefolius*). This herb eases the pain of fibromyalgia.

- Stinging nettle (*Urtica dioica*). Used by herbalists to treat migraine headaches.

- Kava kava (*Piper methysticum*). Use kava kava for tension headaches and neuropathic pain.

- Valerian (*Valeriana officinalis*). Use the root for spasms and muscle cramps.

- Willow (*Salix* spp.). The bark contains salicin, a component in the common pain-relieving drug aspirin (acetylsalicylic acid). If you're allergic to aspirin, don't take salicin-rich willow; as with aspirin, do not give willow to children.

Anti-Inflammatory Herbs (see also page 195)

- Turmeric (*Curcuma longa*). Use fresh or powdered.

- Ginger (*Zingiber officinale*). Best to use fresh.

PAIN POWER HERB:
Skullcap (*Scutellaria lateriflora*)

No matter if your pain is strictly physical (in tissue, bone, or muscle) or if it is neuropathic, you must act to relieve it immediately. Most chronic pain is lodged in the invisible hydra of the nerves, and research is discovering that pain and depression share the same neural pathways. These pathways can become deeply rutted chronic pain channels that are difficult to reverse. Many power herbs are allies for relieving chronic neural pain, including Cannabis, which partners well with skullcap. Skullcap acts to quiet the nervous system. Make a tincture (page 32) from activated Cannabis and skullcap dried leaf (see Resources on page 210), and take 1 teaspoon in juice or water four to six times per day. For an even more powerful pain combination, steep equal parts skullcap, St. John's wort, oatstraw, and Cannabis for a tincture that is effective if your pain stems from the nervous system.

SLEEP

Whether from anxiety, pain, overstimulation, or simply too much caffeine, insomnia affects about 10 percent of people under 40, causing over $100 billion annually in lost productivity. See "Teas to Ease into Sleep," page 176 and try the following tips for creating a sleep-friendly routine.

Tips for Sleep

- Aim to go to bed in a totally dark room at the same time every night.

- Get 20 to 30 minutes of exercise every day and, if you sit at a screen all day, plan to get up and move for 5 minutes every hour or so.

- Avoid caffeine and nicotine late in the day, and abstain from alcohol before bedtime.

- Take a high-CBD–low-THC, indica-dominant strain of Cannabis about one to two hours before bedtime. Start with a low dose (2.5 mg) and add another 2.5 mg the next night until you find the right amount to gently bring on sleep.

- Stop watching screens (TV, phone, iPad, computer) at least an hour before sleep, and keep all screens out of the bedroom.

- Don't lie in bed awake. Try reading or listening to music until you feel drowsy.

- Research the importance of human circadian rhythm to sleep.

Recommended Ratio

Try indica strains with a slightly higher CBD (9 to 13 percent) to THC (6 to 10 percent) ratio. Look for a strain that contains significant amounts of CBN, and pair Cannabis with the hormone melatonin when sleep patterns are disturbed, or with 5-HTP or other power herbs, such as chamomile, lavender, and valerian root, which also contain terpenes found in Cannabis but in much higher concentrations.

NOTE: Melatonin—a hormone, not an herb—is available as a supplement. Use it when your natural sleep pattern is disrupted.

Recommended Foods

- Magnesium-rich foods, such as whole grains, dark leafy greens, black beans, almonds, cashews, pumpkin seeds, salmon, and yogurt, help decrease cortisol, which contributes to insomnia.
- Bananas, cherries, flaxseeds, orange bell peppers, and raspberries contribute melatonin, which helps to control sleep-wake cycles.
- Bananas, kiwis, pecans, pineapples, plums, tomatoes, and walnuts are high in serotonin, which can improve sleep.
- About an hour before bedtime, eat a carbohydrate snack, such as one of my Almond Squares (page 82), Fruit, Nut, and Seed Gems (page 91), or Canna Nut Goof Balls (page 83). Carbohydrates help release tryptophan that is stored in the body and boost serotonin levels.
- Tryptophan-rich foods include turkey, chicken, fish, eggs, and quinoa. Tryptophan is an amino acid that is a precursor of the neurotransmitter serotonin, known as the "feel-good hormone."
- Vitamin B_6 is important to utilizing tryptophan and serotonin, so include avocados, bananas, bulgur, quinoa, pistachios, salmon, brown rice, and sesame seeds in your diet.

Foods to Avoid

- Except for a small carbohydrate snack (see above), avoid eating a meal up to four hours before bedtime.
- Caffeine is a stimulant, so eliminate coffee or tea, cola drinks, and chocolate, or experiment to see if you can take them very early in the morning with no noticeable effect.
- Alcohol and tobacco disrupt sleep.

Recommended Herbs to Promote Sleep

Pair Cannabis with one power herb from the list below:

- Chamomile (*Matricaria recutita*). Chamomile is a traditional sedative that is safe for children. Most commonly taken as a tea for insomnia, it contains the antioxidant apigenin, which relieves the chronic inability to sleep. Chamomile also eases restlessness and irritability. The blue chamomile essential oil can be added to a nighttime bath to soothe the nerves.

- Lavender (*Lavandula* spp.). Use lavender as a gentle tonic for the nervous system. Take as a tea or add to bathwater. Use it in massage oil.
- Lemon balm (*Melissa officinalis*). Lemon balm helps soothe restlessness and insomnia.
- Passionflower (*Passiflora* spp.). This gentle herb is safe for children and people with compromised health and can be used for long periods. It helps ease mental worry, overwork, or nervous exhaustion. It sedates and relaxes you enough to keep you from waking frequently, and it has no lingering effects, leaving you refreshed in the morning.
- Valerian (*Valeriana officinalis*). My experience with this herb is that it helps you to relax and become drowsy about 20 minutes to an hour after taking it, but its effect dwindles if you miss the window. It can encourage wild dreams and, in a very few people, it prevents sleep. Take it for short periods (no more than a month) and use another herb (any in the list above) for a while before using valerian again.

SLEEP POWER HERB:
Ashwagandha (*Withania somnifera*)

As an adaptogen, ashwagandha has the ability to help us cope with stress by replenishing vital energy and restoring strength. Due to its ability to calm or delay a spike in cortisol, the hormone that is triggered by anxiety, ashwagandha helps you fall asleep and get back to sleep if you wake during the night or early in the morning.

Use it as a daily tonic alone or in addition to the herbs in the list on pages 201–202.

Add ashwagandha to the Canna Tincture (pages 33–34).

CAUTION: Do not take ashwagandha with prescription medications, such as benzodiazepines or antidepressants. Also, do not take it if you're pregnant.

< How Cannabis Raises Our Spirits >

Humans (*Homo sapiens*) and the Cannabaceae family (*Cannabis sativa*, *C. indica*, and *C. ruderalis*) have always coexisted. In a sense, we grew up together, developing a long, cooperative relationship. Indeed, Cannabis is our plant ally, as we co-evolve on Earth. Teacher and writer Stephen Gray suggests that the plant may have appeared on the planet as early as 34 million years ago and that it's possible that we began to use it around 12,000 years ago.

Cannabis and other entheogens—plants that alter humans' states of consciousness for religious or spiritual purposes—have a very long history. From Taoism, Zoroastrianism, Hinduism, Buddhism, Sikhism, Christianity, and Judaism to New World cultures, ancient and modern-day shamans, seers, and mystics have and continue to use Cannabis as an incense and/or an edible or inhalant in religious rites and ceremonies aimed at achieving wisdom, self-awareness, and enlightenment.

REFLECTION AND PROJECTION

When used with intention, humility, and respect, Cannabis introduces us to the receptive energy of the yin (feminine) so that we shift into another way of perceiving, thinking, and feeling. With Cannabis as a plant ally, we perceive the material world (or the outer, physical reality) for what it is—an illusion. Through ritual and purposeful intention, Cannabis acts as a spiritual guide. In this way, reflection brings conscious awareness of our oneness, our whole and complete connection to each other, to Earth, and to

God. Cannabis helps us think in nonhabitual ways and open to our deep connection with nature, each other, and our own intuitive heart.

But, you say, Cannabis amplifies the chatter in your head to the point where you're often overwhelmed and begin to panic, feel paranoia, and, sometimes, persecution. I know these effects firsthand. Centuries of spiritual use teach that intention is the key to directing Cannabis toward inviting peaceful stillness and allowing space for

< 203 >

contemplation and reflection. Finding the perfect strain and ratio of CBD to THC that works for you is also helpful in determining the outcome of every experience. Cannabis summons us to dream, create, and explore the nonmaterial world of pure, life-supporting energy.

IT STARTS WITH RESPECT AND MOVES INTO STILLNESS

It's not always about us. If we were to shift gears from head to heart, we'd be incredibly grateful and hold plants (not just Cannabis, but all plants and sentient beings) in high esteem, recognizing their authentic vibration, wisdom, and ability to open our hearts.

In Buddhist teaching, *shunyata*, or "emptiness," is peace. Becoming aware or awakening the observer invokes love. Unless we can do this, we are doomed to continue along the path toward the destruction and ultimate exhaustion of the planet's gifts.

Clearly, Cannabis helps the mind, body, and spirit. In *The Benefits of Marijuana*, Joan Bello reminds us that: "Medicinal, recreational, and sacramental utilization of this plant are actually identical. To be healthy is to be happy is to be holy, all of which are connected with Cannabis use."

Dee Dussault, in her article "For the Love of the Leaf" in Stephen Gray's *Cannabis and Spirituality*, advises that: "Cannabis is not the moon, but it can be a finger pointing at the moon, and this is its great value."

RITUAL IN THE GARDEN AND KITCHEN

Throughout the growing season, I commune with my plants and harvest their flowers and leaves with a brief prayer—always with respect and gratitude. When I work with any herb, I start with impeccably clean tools and a spotless kitchen, I give thanks to the herb for its gifts, and I use the time spent preparing the herb as a working meditation. I envision the infused oil or tincture as having the highest healing ability. I sometimes sing, and I always engage with the process from my heart.

When it comes time to use the Cannabis infusion in a recipe, again, I call on the highest spiritual intentions, those of love, peace, or connection as I make the edibles I've developed for this book.

No matter if you are simply curious about Cannabis or if your goal is to be well or to seek enlightenment, no matter if you want to ease pain or inflammation, whatever your intention, I hope you enter into a mindful and disciplined walk with Cannabis.

Glossary

adaptogen   An herb that helps the body resist stress and restore balance to body systems.

analgesic   An herb that relieves pain.

anti-inflammatory   A substance in plants that reduces swelling in the body.

anthocyanins   Part of the flavonoid group of pigments that appear in red, purple, blue, or black plants. Anthocyanins are both antioxidant and anti-inflammatory, two of the most important factors in preventing diseases.

antioxidant   A phytonutrient found in plants that destroys aging- and disease-promoting free radicals.

antispasmodic   An herb that helps relax muscle cramps.

cannabinoids   The chemicals that give the Cannabis plant its medicinal and recreational properties.

Cannabis   An ancient, healing annual herb; the dried flower buds of the plant have been called "marijuana."

CBD   Short for "cannabidiol," a Cannabis cannabinoid that may hold the most promise for healing.

decarboxylation   The heating process (via smoking, vaping, cooking) that causes the THCA (tetrahydrocannabinolic acid) and CBDA (cannabidiolic acid) in raw Cannabis plants to turn into THC and CBD (see respective Glossary entries).

decoction   A method of extracting active, medicinal ingredients from the woody parts of herbs by boiling them in a covered container of water for 5 to 20 minutes. A decoction is sometimes steeped with the plant material in a covered container for 10 minutes to 48 hours after boiling.

endocannabinoids   Components, mostly fatty acids produced by the human body, similar in structure to cannabinoids found in Cannabis plants.

endocannabinoid system (ECS)   The body's receptors that allow the intake of cannabinoids, especially THC and CBD.

essential oil   The oil found in aerial parts of herbs that is extracted by distillation; active constituents are concentrated in these oils, which are usually blended with almond or other plant oils before being applied topically. Use caution before taking pure essential oils internally.

< 205 >

flavonoids	Constituents of plants whose primary benefits to the plants are to filter out UV rays, help attract pollinators, discourage pests, and provide pigmentation (color). For humans, flavonoids are important because they help to prevent diseases.
ganja	Another word for Cannabis; derived from the Sanskrit word for "hemp," *gañjā*.
ghee	Butter that has been clarified by simmering over heat (see page 17). The milk solids sink to the bottom of the fats and can be strained out, leaving pure, bright yellow fatty acids.
glycemic index	The glycemic index (GI) ranks foods according to their metabolization rate due to the nature and amount of carbohydrates in them. For example, foods with a low GI value (55 or less) are called complex carbohydrates because the carbohydrate is bound in fiber, which causes them to be more slowly digested, absorbed into the bloodstream, and converted to energy (metabolized). High GI foods (with a rating above 55) cause a faster rise in blood glucose (sugar) levels, which can be challenging for diabetics.
hashish	The resin of the Cannabis plant.
hemp	Strains of *Cannabis sativa* that have been bred specifically for fiber for clothing and construction, oils and topical ointment, and nutritional supplements; it has a 0.3 percent THC limit (see also THC).
hybrid	In Cannabis botany, a heterozygous plant resulting from crossing two separate strains.
hybridization	The process of crossing differing gene pools to produce offspring of combined parental characteristics.
indica	A primary species of Cannabis, typically associated with full-body, relaxing effects and helping to improve sleep and alleviate pain.
infusion	The process by which active ingredients from herbs are drawn out into water, oil (fat), alcohol, vinegar, salt, or sugar.
maca	Sometimes called a superfood, the root of a plant called maca (*Lepidium meyenii*) is usually dried, ground and added to drinks or raw cookies or "bites." It may help boost energy and increase strength and stamina.
marijuana	*See* Cannabis.
neurodegenerative diseases	Diseases where a progressive loss of the functions of neurons in the brain cause many different symptoms including Alzheimer's disease, Parkinson's disease, Tourette's syndrome, Huntington's disease, HIV/AIDS, dementia, Down syndrome, and heart disease.
oxidation, oxidative stress	Stress and toxins from the environment, smoking, or from food and drink cause the formation of free radicals (unstable, oxygen-containing molecules) in the body, which can harm cells and speed ageing. See also Antioxidants.
pharmacopoeia	A list of often plant-based medicinal ingredients and chemicals issued by an officially recognized authority and serving as a standard for pharmacists and doctors.

psychoactive	A plant or drug that affects the consciousness or psyche.
sativa	A primary species of Cannabis, typically associated with cerebral and energizing effects; sometimes associated with higher THC than indica-dominant Cannabis species.
strain	A variety of plant developed by breeding.
sublingual	Herbalists and medical caregivers often advise that medicines in tincture form be taken under the tongue (sublingually), which allows the active constituents to bypass the digestive system and enter the bloodstream through the vessel-rich tissues within the sublingual cavity.
terpenes	A group of hydrocarbons found in the essential oils of plants, produced alongside cannabinoids, that provide smell and taste and have their own medicinal properties.
terpenoids	Terpenes are phytonutrients that have been dried and cured or chemically modified.
THC	Short for "tetrahydrocannabinol," the principal (and most famous) psychoactive cannabinoid in Cannabis.
tincture	A concentrated medicinal preparation of fresh or dried herb in alcohol, glycerine, or vinegar.
trichomes	Small glands on the stalk, leaf, and flower of Cannabis that secrete psychoactive chemicals from resins produced by the trichomes.
warming herbs	Herbs that, when ingested, elicit a warming sensation by bringing blood to the surface of the skin, which, in turn, raises the temperature or heats it. (e.g., ginger, cinnamon, cayenne, and garlic, along with some green herbs such as rosemary).
whole spectrum	When herbal oils, tinctures, or extractions are made from the whole herb, and thus contain all the healing constituents that were present in the herb, they are called "whole-spectrum preparations." Herbalists work with whole plant medicine because of the synergistic actions of all of the components while pharmacists extract one constituent for what is called an isolate or drug.

< **Acknowledgments** >

For me, Cannabis is a magic herb, full of potential for healing and well-being. I'm grateful to teachers like Tammy Sweet, Rosemary Gladstar, Conrad Richter, the late Art Tucker, Rex Talbert, Matt and Andrea Reisen, the late Jim Duke, and Chuck Voigt, who continue to inspire and help me understand the power and rich complexities of all herbs.

Sterling publishes great books, and I'm proud to be one of their authors. I'm in awe and so appreciative of the whole publishing team who work hard to bring those books into beautiful reality–to Jennifer Williams for your sensitivity and vision; word wizards Diana Drew and Renee Yewdaev; designer Shannon Plunkett, who works miracles in bringing words to life; and marketing ninja Blanca Oliviery, who is exceptional at promotion. Thanks to the keen eye of Jo Obarowski, creative director, and Chris Bain's impeccable work as photo director, the recipes virtually take shape on the pages. Cover designer, Igor Satanovsky's brilliant work wraps every talented contribution into a beautiful package. Fond appreciation goes to Linda Konner, my matchless agent.

To my passionate herb support group— Marion Bardman, Susan Belsinger, Susan Betz, Gert Coleman, Gayle Engles, Jane Hawley-Stevens, Gloria Hunter, Pat Kenny, Theresa Mieseler, Gudrun Penselin, Lori Schaeffer, Holly Shimizu, Skye Suter, and Tina Marie Wilcox—your knowledge and love of herbs makes knowing and sharing time with you a joyful experience.

Love and gratitude to my home team, Gary McLaughlin, Shannon McLaughlin, and Leanne Milech.

< 208 >

< **Bibliography** >

Bello, Joan. *The Benefits of Marijuana: Physical, Psychological, and Spiritual.* Cottonwood, CA: Sweetlight Books, 1996.

Bingham, Roy. "5 Recipes for Sweet Success in the Cannabis Candy Market.": Green Entrepreneur. https://www.greenentrepreneur.com/article/316791.

Dussault, Dee. "For the Love of the Leaf," in Stephen Gray, ed., *Cannabis and Spirituality: An Explorer's Guide to an Ancient Plant Spirit Ally.* Rochester, VT: Park Street Press, 2017, 117–128.

Gray, Stephen, ed. *Cannabis and Spirituality: An Explorer's Guide to an Ancient Plant Spirit Ally.* Rochester, VT: Park Street Press, 2017.

FURTHER READING

Anderson, Dr. Paul, and Dr. Mark Stengler. *Outside the Box: Cancer Therapies.* Carlsbad, CA: Hay House Inc., 2018.

Courtney, Dr. William. "Cannabis as a Unique Functional Food: Impact of THC on Dietary Intake of Cannabinoid Acids," https://www.cannabisinternational.org/info/treatingyourself.pdf

Flowers: The Art of Rocky Mountain Cannabis. Calgary, Alberta, Canada: Stray Books Ltd., 2019.

Ivker, Dr. Rav. *Cannabis for Chronic Pain: A Proven Prescription for Using Marijuana to Relieve Your Pain and Heal Your Life.* New York: Touchstone Books, 2017.

Leafly Team. *The Leafly Guide to Cannabis.* New York: Twelve, Hachette Book Group, 2017.

O'Leary-Randall, Alice. *Medical Marijuana in America: Memoir of a Pioneer.* Middleton, DE: Self-published, Createspace, 2014.

< 209 >

< **Resources** >

MEDICINAL HERB SUPPLIERS

- Healing Spirits Herb Farm (www.healingspiritsherbfarm.com): organic, bulk, dried herbs

- Mountain Rose Herbs (www.mountainroseherbs.com): high-quality dried herbs

- Organic Connections (www.orgcon.ca): organic, bulk, dried herbs and spices

- Richters Herbs (www.richters.com): seeds, plants, some dried herbs

- Nova Decarboxylator by Ardent (www.ardentcannabis.com): A device that automatically decarboxylates raw cannabis. It is often used by people who live in shared accommodation, condominiums, or apartments because it diminishes odors from the process.

< **Photography Credits** >

Pat Crocker: 74, 90, 149, 152, 172, 184, 185

Getty images: Anton Belo 70, Creative-Family 23, EasterBunnyUK 98, Veselova Elena 127, Furo Felix 61, Dmitrii Ivanov 178, Jenifoto 112, Kobeza 100, Nadezhda Nesterova 129, Lew Robertson i-ii, viii, 48, 50, 58, 77, 104, 138, 164, Asha Sathees Photography 12, Simarik 181, VankaD 168, Wmaster890 56

Bill Milne: 55, 64, 74, 84, 86, 90, 92, 111, 118, 120, 123, 125, 132, 136, 142, 144, 149, 152, 156, 163

Shutterstock: Nataliya Arzamasova 115, Natasha Breen 17, Poring Studio 40, Tanya Sid 22

< 210 >

< **Index** >

Note: Page numbers in *italics* indicate recipes.

< **211** >

< About the Author >

Pat Crocker's mission in life is to write with insight and experience, cook with playful abandon, and eat with gusto. She is the author of 22 cookbooks, with more than 1.25 million copies in print and several translated into a dozen languages. Crocker holds a degree in Food, Nutrition, Consumer, and Family Studies from Ryerson University, Toronto, and has been honored twice, as a culinary herbalist, with the International Herb Association's Professional Award. In 2009, Crocker received the Gertrude H. Foster award from the Herb Society of America for Excellence in Herbal Literature. Her books, *The Juicing Bible* and *The Vegan Cook's Bible* (both published

CREDIT: GARY MCLAUGHLIN

by Robert Rose) have won Best in the World awards from the International Gourmand Culinary Guild. *The Herbalist's Kitchen* (Sterling, 2018) earned Silver in the Health category from Taste Canada.

Pat Crocker has honed her herb practice over more than four decades of growing, studying, photographing, experimenting with, and writing about what she calls, *the helping plants*. In fact, Crocker infuses the medicinal benefits of herbs in every original recipe she develops. Pat began exploring and cooking with Cannabis to help her husband find relief from chronic back pain. To learn more about Pat Crocker, visit patcrocker.com.